"The arguments of Judge Douglas are about as thin as homeopathic soup made by boiling the shadow of a pigeon that had starved to death"

— *A. Lincoln.*

Bill's Blogs

Copyright © 2016 Hawkhill Assoc., Inc.
All rights reserved.

ISBN-13: 9781559791984
ISBN-10: 1559791985

A note on the title: originally the working title of this book was "Bill's Fuckin' Blogs. I lost my nerve after some complaints and changed it to the simpler "Bill's Blogs." I am in my ninetieth year on this planet. I seldom use profanity and almost never use the F-word. I am not always consistent. My wife's is a few years older than I, has more courage and a more contemporary vocabulary. She regularly edits my weekly blogs and at times has made it known that sometimes she resents my spending so much time on them. In a moment of frustration she once said, "You don't pay enough attention to me—you just go on writing those fuckin' blogs."

In defense, I showed her the recent New Yorker cartoon that has Shakespeare sitting next to a pretty girl who is holding up the page of a new manuscript. The pretty girl is not impressed: "Wow, another sonnet."

Jane is a fan of the New Yorker. Not so much of Shakespeare.

In the end we agreed that Bill's Fuckin' Blogs was a decent title for this collection. But later as I explained I lost my nerve and on advice from a few friends and editors changed it the present more vanilla title which they thought would be more saleable. We'll see.

Oh, the Days Dwindle Down to a Precious Few

● ● ●

Dec. 14, 2015

> September, November,
> And these few precious days I'll spend with you,
> These precious days I'll spend with you!

I USED TO LIKE THE fall but now not so much. School begins. I'm not that interested anymore. And with my poor hearing, I can't understand what the professors are saying anyway. Football and other sports are fun to watch, but I can't play. Leaves are pretty but a nuisance to rake. The days get so short in Wisconsin; the dark comes before you even have time to think about that drink before supper.

When you get as old as my wife and me (90 and 93 respectively), you can always just wait to die. The Welsh poet Dylan Thomas advises:

> Do not go gentle into that good night
> Old age should burn and rave at close of day
> Rage, rage against the dying of the light.

I'm a little like the old guy who raged because he had no shoes until he met a man who had no feet. I've led a comfortable life and have no cause for complaint. I flatter myself that I have made a significant contribution to society with my thoughts and writings on societal evolution—Hunting/Gathering to Agricultural to Modern (see the next chapter, "Philosophy"). Maybe even with Bill's Laws (see chapter following the next) as well as my video programs in science and democratic history (go to YouTube and look up "Bill Stonebarger.")

Some customers agree. A few even consider me "one of the finest minds of the century" (full disclosure: my daughter-in-law, two sisters, and some fans in the UK, Europe, and South Africa).

Like Winston Churchill, I too believe, "We are all worms. But I do believe that I am a glow-worm." In spite of all that bragging, I'm a little down this solstice season.

Jane and I watched a TV special last night celebrating the one-hundredth birthday of Frank Sinatra (Frank actually died at eighty-three). Sinatra was a favorite of mine. I could understand his words, and I liked his songs, which is more than I can say for most pop singers and songs today. I was put off by the glitter and showbiz schmaltz of the birthday special, but I enjoyed the music.

I was also a wee bit envious. I have never been that keen on fame and fortune. But I do think modern celebrities like Sinatra, as well as many pop music and sport stars, are overrated and overpraised. They make too much money, besides. They can be fun for a while, but they don't last. Who remembers the entertainment and sports stars of my youth? Jack Benny? Bob Hope? Rita Hayworth? Lana Turner? Tommy Dorsey? Glenn Miller? Amos 'n Andy? Stepin Fetchit? Johnny Vander Meer (who pitched the only consecutive no-hit games for the Cincinnati Reds)? The Four Horsemen (the Notre Dame football ones)? The Brown Bomber Joe Louis (my family and I listened to all his heavyweight championship fights on the radio during the depression)? Even Babe Ruth and Lou Gehrig of the Yankees—or was it the Red Sox?

On the other hand, scientists, philosophers, composers, artists, industrialists, politicians, and authors from ages past, like Sophocles, Aquinas, Newton, Shakespeare, da Vinci, Hume, Bach, Mozart, Darwin, Smith, Marx, Jefferson, Washington, Lincoln, Carnegie, Rockefeller, Pasteur,

Edison, Thoreau, Twain, or Dickinson, are remembered because their work has lasted. This is also true of tens of thousands of other achievers who have contributed to Modern Age culture.

Curiously and sadly, it may not be true for many of today's famous and accomplished Western scientists, professors, politicians, authors, artists, and musicians who make up what I call the *modern clergy*—people like Barack and Michelle Obama, Bernie Sanders, Hillary and Bill Clinton, Al Gore, Elizabeth Warren, Joe Biden, George Bush, John McCain, Jimmy Carter, Richard Nixon, Eric Holder, Paul Ehrlich, John Holdren, Al Gore, Bill McKibben, Paul Krugman, George Soros, Warren Buffett, Jeffrey Immelt, Michael Bloomberg, Bill Gates, Steven Spielberg, Al Sharpton, Steven Colbert, Dan Rather, Noam Chomsky, Whoopi Goldberg, Beyoncé Knowles-Carter, Paul Newman, Oprah Winfrey, Robert Redford, or the departed FDR, LBJ, Walter Cronkite, Edward R. Murrow, Arthur Miller, Rachel Carson, Ernest Hemingway, Bertrand Russell, Jean-Paul Sartre, Steve Jobs, Berthold Brecht, Howard Zinn, Pablo Picasso, Jackson Pollock, Leonard Bernstein, John Lennon, Muhammad Ali, and many, many others.

Most of these modern experts knock the Modern Age that has nurtured them and few find the United States exceptional for starting it. Many are famous for making foolish predictions or supporting reactionary (fascist and socialist) fixes for modern problems. Some win Nobel or Pulitzer Prizes, and are certainly talented, but to my mind most get too much fame, fortune, and followers.

Immodestly, I put myself in the first class. Not with Newton, Darwin, or Jefferson, but with the tens of thousand of other achievers who contributed to and appreciated the Modern Age. In short, I think I do deserve more credit than I get for my blogs and videos. They may not rise to the Darwinian or Jeffersonian level, but they are a step above the contemporary theatrical, sport, entertainment, and pop music contributions that get so much acclaim and money today.

I'm not exactly sure where this is heading—maybe to my latest idea for a book—this one, *Bill's Fuckin' Blogs*. Maybe this time I'll get lucky: the book will be a hit and give me the critical fame I richly deserve…and more cash.

Philosophy

● ● ●

Oct. 12, 2015

I BEGAN MY PHILOSOPHIC QUEST eighty-some years ago. I was a *good* boy who took seriously the lessons of nuns and priests in Catholic schools. I paid attention to my Catholic catechism when it asked what I thought at the time was the all-important question, "Why are we here?" And I believed its no-nonsense answer: "We are here to do good so that we can win an eternity of happiness with God in heaven. If we are bad, though, we will suffer an eternity of punishment in hell."

Something close to that—I couldn't find the version that I remember on the Internet.

Besides being a good boy, I was also a straight-A student who seldom read beyond the teacher's assignments. I'm pretty sure the nuns had me pegged early along for the priesthood. Fortunately, my father was opposed, and for that I thank him posthumously. It was later in the navy and in college that I began my self-education by reading serious history, science, and idea books of my own choosing. It was the start of my personal Renaissance, Reformation, and Enlightenment.

In my personal Renaissance and Reformation, I became a bleeding-heart liberal. I still have a bleeding heart, but now I am liberal only in the classic *freedom* sense of Washington, Adams, and Jefferson. Otherwise, I class myself as a libertarian Republican. My first marriage was in a college Friends chapel with a ceremony we composed ourselves. I thought then that

I had permanently left the church, but I soon learned it wasn't that easy. Like giving up smoking, I had more than one relapse. I remember vividly the time in college when I retreated to nearby woods and sobbed uncontrollably for my immortal soul in front of a crude crucifix I made of twigs.

Later I got my master's degree in philosophy from New York University with a thesis on the *self*—a synonym, I thought then for *soul*. I read Enlightenment philosophers like David Hume and American pragmatists like William James and John Dewey. The American pragmatist of some fame as well, Sidney Hook, was my thesis adviser. They all convinced me that, like Bucky Fuller once wrote that, "I seem to be a verb." *Soul*, I concluded, was a leftover (a meme) from our medieval past. In my personal Enlightenment, I became an atheist like many of our Founding Fathers. I remain so today.

The truth is I was never that thrilled with academic philosophy. When I was at NYU graduate school in the early 1950s, at center stage were existentialists like Jean-Paul Sartre competing with logical positivists like Bertrand Russell. If anything, I tended to side with the existentialists, being then something of a left-liberal beatnik. A good friend at the time compared me to Jack Kerouac.

I had problems with one course, Symbolic Logic. It never seemed to relate to my spiritual quest. I had always been good in math, but math, too, seemed useful only to teach later. Later of course it turned out that symbolic logic was the intellectual mathematical base for digital computing! Symbolic logic along with some mathematician tricks gave birth to Apple, Microsoft, Facebook, the Internet, and the like. Jeepers! Gosh, if only I had paid more attention then and had better judgment like Marlon Brando in the 1954 hit movie *On the Waterfront*, "I coulda been a contender." And rich man like Bill Gates.

I have gone through many stages in my long life, both painful and progressive. To support my family and myself, I taught school. I was not a born teacher. All the time I was teaching, I also wrote poetry in the early morning and for a longer spell worked in theater: acting, directing, and writing. My significant contribution to the world of ideas came late.

I stumbled upon it in my sixties, seventies, eighties, and after a lifetime of reading in science, history, and philosophy. Here is a summary.

Historians sometimes divide human history into three major ages—the Hunting/Gathering, the Agricultural, and our own Modern Age. Each age came with unprecedented growth in available resources, exploding populations, and new challenges. The division is not original with me, but in my reading so far, few, if any, thinkers have used these facts to gain insights into the Modern Age.

I claim the Modern Age as the result of three historical trends: (1) an explosive growth of science and technology, (2) freedom of and from religion, and (3) free-market capitalism. All three merged synergistically in the late eighteenth century with the founding of a new nation-state, the United States. I claim this is what we mean—or at least we *should* mean—when we call this country *exceptional*. This is what Abraham Lincoln meant when he called the United States, "the last best hope of earth."

The Hunting/Gathering was the longest age, more than a hundred thousand years. It included the evolution of *Homo sapiens*. In a few places on Earth—the Amazon basin, Africa, Australia, and South Pacific Islands—some human tribes still live in that Hunting/Gathering Age. Many Modern Age communities and individuals, including our own, have hand-me-downs (memes) left over from this age: tattoos, body jewelry, primitive music, dancing, art, and environmental myths.

The Agricultural Age began around ten thousand years ago. It is still with us in many places and ways. Memes, like genes, don't change easily. The Agricultural Age saw the birth of cities, civilizations, and the birth of most modern religions: Pagan, Buddhist, Hindu, Confucian, and the three monotheistic ones—Judaism, Christianity, and Islam. *Many* political, social, religious, and psychological memes from this age survive today, and many societies today, including our own, are firmly stuck in some of the reactionary memes of this Agricultural Age.

Some ideas and patterns of thought (memes) inherited from the Western Christian version of the Agricultural Age are good and desirable: individualism, romantic love, forgiveness, tolerance, charity, family, private property, logic, reason, the beginnings of science , the beginnings of capitalism, care for the Earth, and compassion for the poor and handicapped.

Some memes from both earlier ages are also still common today in both the West and the East and are bad and reactionary. The single most important of these is seeing wealth as static and fixed—specifically in the Agricultural Age as land, gold, and slaves (in the Hunting / Gathering version, wealth was prime hunting-and-gathering land). In other words, seeing wealth and resources as a big pie—true, if you get more, I am certain to get less.

Other reactionary memes follow logically and reasonably from this key one: settling differences with war; imperialism and exploitation of the weak; equating honor with male violence; keeping females submissive in the home and marketplace; arranging marriages to increase status and wealth; distrusting strangers and all minorities; seeing exclusive supernatural religions as a refuge from chaos and violence; using wealth and status to prejudge people and to justify slavery, serfdom, peasantry, caste, and all class divisions; creating authoritarian, tyrannical, monarchial, or totalitarian governments in futile attempts to bring more equality and justice; and in recent times using love of nature to justify reactionary economic policies and using *organic* and *natural* concepts to justify back-to-Earth, anti-science, anti-technology, socialist, and *sustainable* movements; and so forth.

All of which helps explain my opposition to the present pope and his Western Progressive and Green friends (which in past times have included me). In most cases they, perhaps unknowingly, support reactionary Agricultural or Hunting/Gathering memes. In other words, Pope Francis and Green-Progressives of the Democratic Party are not the true *progressive* leaders we need to cope with the unique challenges of the Modern Age.

Parker and Bill's Laws

● ● ●

Jan. 4, 2015

A BREATH OF FRESH AIR just blew through our house. Our tenants (and friends), Pierce and Robin Edmiston, have been renting the second-floor apartment of our house on East Gilman Street. They just had a baby girl. They named her Parker.

What will Parker's life be like thirty years from now?

This is a tougher question than I addressed before, what the world would be like five hundred years from now [see the next entry in this book]. If Obama and his chief science adviser, John Holdren, are right, then the future for Parker looks grim. Physicist Holdren, for instance, was one of the scientists who predicted on the first Earth Day in 1970 that "if present trends continue the world in 2000 will be more crowded, more polluted, less stable ecologically and more vulnerable to disruption than the world we live in now. Serious stresses involving population, resources, and environment are clearly visible ahead. Despite greater material output, the world's people will be poorer in many ways than they are today."[1]

Judging by his recent speeches, our President Obama would say the same about the world in 2045, thirty years from now (at least he warned of this outcome unless we elect more Progressive-Green Democrats like himself).

---

1 Ed. Simon and Kahn. *The Resourceful Earth* (1984).

One of Holdren's partners in that first Earth Day prediction, biologist and butterfly expert Paul Ehrlich went further. He predicted that due to overpopulation, millions of Americans would starve before the twentieth century ended. He also predicted that the United Kingdom might not exist and wrote that India and China were both doomed basket cases. They were in fact so hopeless all we could do was triage and watch helplessly while millions of Indians and Chinese starved to death.

In the same vein, in 2007 an international panel of scientists warned that increasing levels of carbon dioxide in the atmosphere would bring global climate change and worldwide catastrophe as temperatures soared, glaciers melted, sea levels rose, cities were flooded, islands disappeared, species went extinct, rain patterns changed, and warm-weather diseases become pandemic. According to these experts, we are in for a truly apocalyptic catastrophe.

Like predictions of some religious groups, none of this has happened yet. But just you wait! From the Shakers to Jim Jones to Y2K to Jehovah's Witnesses to Heaven's Gate to Muslim terrorists to secular Doomsters today, true believers in all these religions have placed their bets (in some cases their very lives) on apocalyptic fears and hopes.

In honor of these true believers, on my daily swim last week, I made up some new laws. Call them Bill's Laws.

1. A bad idea in modern science has a half-life of about ten years.
2. A bad idea in modern politics has a half-life of about a hundred years.
3. A bad idea in modern religion has a half-life of about a thousand years.

What will this mean for Parker in thirty years?

Many bad-idea apocalyptic scientific scares about population and resources began in the late 1960s. According to my first law, they should be played out by now. They pretty much are. Like earlier enthusiasm for ideas like eugenics, Freudian analysis, racism and sexism, few scientists take them seriously now. (Note: President Woodrow Wilson and

Planned Parenthood founder Margaret Sanger led the way with racism and Germany's leading anti-Semites took their racist ideas seriously enough to act on them with tragic consequences).

As for current science-based ideas like overpopulation, resource scarcity or carbon pollution, admittedly the jury is still out. But does any scientist really believe that *Soylent Green* is likely for New York City seven years from now? (*Soylent Green* was a popular doomster movie of 1973 predicted that, due to overpopulation and rampant pollution, the poor in NYC of 2022 would be reduced to eating the only food available, wafers of Soylent Green, advertised as made from seaweed but actually made from corpses!)

Does any scientist claim now that China's large population, resource shortages and potential climate change will be a fatal handicap to its growth and wealth? How many couples in the modern world follow the green advice, "save the Earth, don't give birth"? How many communities or individuals really believe and follow the advice of the bumper sticker, "a growing economy means a shrinking ecosystem?"

Despite the support of Obama, Pope Francis, and the United Nations, I predict that global warming (aka climate change) is yet another bad idea in science. It will have the same short life span as former bad ideas about eugenics, psychoanalysis, racism, sexism, population, and resource shortages had a few decades ago. Remember, the vast majority of scientists, politicians along with a gullible public, supported all of these just a few decades ago.

True, in geologic history a warmer Earth did come with increasing CO_2, but the increases *followed* the warming, so that could not have been the cause. In short, no matter how much carbon dioxide we add to air, it is unlikely to warm us much in the next thirty or one hundred years.

My bet is that Bill's Law will prove valid, and Parker will not suffer from rising sea levels, coastal flooding, overpopulated cities or countries, lost islands, species going extinct, excessive heat and pollution, or shortages of energy or of any material thing—no matter how long she lives.

She may run into trouble from religious strife, though. The Christian world has, thankfully, already passed through most of its millennial half-lives. No one in the West so far as I know is eager to burn heretics or stone sinners now. Many radicals in the Muslim world still do. Radical Muslims (even many moderate ones) think women should be submissive to their arranged-marriage husbands; crimes like adultery and fornication should be punished by public whipping and stoning; sharia law is the best law and should be adopted universally; many Muslims don't find it ridiculous that Christians, atheists, and, in fact, *all* nonbelievers in Islam should be beheaded or murdered and their killers will be rewarded in heaven for their devotion to Allah. In medieval times this last bad idea in religion—exclusive monotheism—led to many bloody wars and heretic burnings in the Christian world. Today it is doing the same in the Muslim world, and it may get worse. In Europe it already has. America, too, may not always be a safe haven. So we can't rule out the possibility that thirty years from now Parker may meet some bloody times.

What about political ideas that according to Bill's Laws have a half-life of about a century?

Socialism/communism didn't start with the German intellectual Karl Marx, but he gave it a strong intellectual boost. Germany was a leader in charitable social welfare during the nineteenth century. In the twentieth century, the Nazis added racism to the socialist mix (influenced in part by scientific racist ideas in the United States and Europe) bringing on the Holocaust and World War II. Remember, *Nazi* was short for National *Socialist* German Workers Party.) The Nazis and the Italian, Spanish and Japanese fascists were also widely praised—prewar—by some religious adherents in the West for their social-welfare theories and policies. Not, of course, by Jews, gypsies, the aged, the handicapped, and gays, who suffered grievously. Also note that citizens who dissented from socialist/communist ideas and policies also suffered grievously in Soviet bloc countries in the twentieth century.

Western intellectuals and politicians have flirted with socialist/communist ideas for more than two centuries now. I claim that bad political ideas have a half-life of about a hundred years. On schedule, socialist/communist ideas are indeed starting to show their age. Socialism was a recipe for catastrophe in Cuba, China, North Korea, Russia, and Soviet bloc countries. It has been responsible for recent sharp declines in wealth and increases in violence in South American countries—Venezuela, Brazil, Argentina, Peru, Bolivia, and Ecuador—that have tried to marry it with democracy. Even many social-welfare democracies in Europe— France, Spain, the United Kingdom, the Netherlands, Belgium, and the Scandinavian countries—are in serious trouble today. These countries do have, as Bernie Sanders takes pains to remind us often: wealth, decent and cheap national health care, generous laws to support vacations, family leave, shorter working days, and other popular social benefits. They also all have stagnant economies; declines of their not-very-diverse-in-the-first-place native populations; unassimilated, radical, and fast-growing Muslim populations; resurgent and often vicious anti-Semitism; high unemployment, especially among the young and minority populations; increasingly bloody terror attacks; and a noticeable decline in science, culture, and technology. They also have such weak defense forces they are forced to rely on the United States to protect them from foreign aggression or internal revolution.

Democratic socialist Bernie Sanders and, perhaps to a slightly lesser extent, establishment Democrats like Hillary Clinton and President Obama, are attempting to bring back socialism today, as FDR did nearly a hundred years ago in the Great Depression. On he other side of the globe, China, India, and many other developing countries have recently abandoned socialism for a more market-oriented economy.

When you subsidize dependence and welfare, you get more dependence and welfare. You also get as unwelcome side effects: a stagnant economy; severe immigration problems; and growing unemployment. They are discovering these side effects in many European countries today. It takes a while—like a hundred years or so according to Bill's Laws.

My guess is that it is time for the genuinely progressive ideas of freedom and self-respect (libertarian ideas of the Adam Smith and Founding Fathers variety) to once again surge to the front and lead the Modern Age. Whether that will happen in the next thirty years is debatable. Five hundred years from now, I see it as inevitable.

Fantasy History from 2515 Tanzania

• • •

Jan. 12, 2015

AN EAST COAST FRIEND CHALLENGED me to predict what the Modern Age would be like five hundred years from now. Here is my answer, translated from the Swahili of a 2515 school history book in Tanzania.

The Modern Age began with the founding of a new idea-based country in North America in the late eighteenth century. In the twentieth century, Europe followed with baby steps into this Modern Age. In the twenty-first century, Asia, the Middle East, and Africa joined the parade. At the beginning of that twenty-first century, there was a period of intense fanaticism and violence as Islamic reform and Enlightenment began, along with a lingering sympathy and commitment to socialism/communism.

A few decades later, Africa took a giant step forward when it discovered new energy resources, reduced its reliance on aid from wealthier countries, and developed export industries like advanced vehicles, fashion clothing, new sports equipment, and digital technology that today have reached maturity and paid rich dividends. Africa has also benefited from a worldwide growth in intelligence and freedom. (The Flynn Effect, discovered in twentieth century America, showed an average advance of three IQ points per decade, especially important and pronounced in the developing countries of Africa.)

By the twenty-third century, the Middle East, Asia, and Africa were all firmly in the Modern Age. Behavior patterns (memes) of past ages were no longer dominant, although many survived in muted forms as they had done for centuries in Western countries. Even though rare now, there were still reports of reactionary memes making a difference. Like: torture; lashing and decapitating criminals, traitors, enemies, and political opponents; making peasants, serfs, and slaves of lower classes; viewing the mentally unbalanced, homosexuals, impoverished, and drug users as criminals; dividing society into semi-permanent classes based on wealth and family history; treating the female half of the population as property; open racism and sexism, even genocidal incidents; using promises of reward and punishment after death, miracles, and charity to keep the masses dependent; using wars to gain more land, gold, and wealth (often with child soldiers); destroying animal and plant species in quest of more natural resources; creating gardens, zoos, and wilderness preserves in atonement; giving excessive obeisance to academic and religious elites; making male honor and disrespect an excuse for violence; making a god of Mother Earth.

In the final decades of changeover to the Modern Age in the twenty-first century, many intellectuals on all continents worried needlessly about the dangers from new technologies, climate change, overpopulation, and resource scarcity, when the real challenges were as always poverty, disease, and ignorance in a world of wonder and plenty.

All of the reactionary patterns (memes) listed above originated either in the ten-thousand-year-long Agricultural Age or in the one-hundred-thousand-year-long Hunting/Gathering Age (when *Homo sapiens* evolved in Africa). Scholars had four theories to explain these major changes in populations, resources, and lifestyles that happened during ages past and for the changes that happened in transition between the ages: Environmental (the environment is always the key factor), Progressive (the haves dominate the have-nots and civilization's rise and fall from failures in leadership); Religious (God commands; humans obey or rebel); and Evolutionary[2] (the view held by most historians today).

The first three had no explanation for the unprecedented growth in population and wealth that came with the Modern Age and the changes brought by the Agricultural Age. Proponents simply reiterated their basic messages: Environmentalists claimed humans were destroying nature even more with technology and that we are more likely to see apocalyptic doom in the future; Progressives claimed the "haves" continued to exploit the "have-nots" in ever more clever and technologic ways, and we are doomed unless we elect more progressive leaders; Religious partisans claim God and sinful humans are at odds still, and we are as always doomed for our sins.

The Evolutionary view lists specific causes for the explosive growth of population and wealth following the transition from hunting and gathering to agricultural: (1) new technology to increase food production and animal husbandry, (2) increase in the density of populations, and (3) increase in intelligence and literacy due to the evolution of *Homo sapiens.*

The Evolution view also lists specific causes for the move from the Agricultural Age to the Modern Age: (1) an explosive growth of science and technology (especially fossil fuel energy and technology); (2) a welcome increase in freedom of thought coming out of the Christian Renaissance, Reformation, and

---

[2] Charles Darwin, a well-known, well-traveled amateur naturalist in England, founded evolutionary science in the nineteenth century. A not-so-well-known though well-traveled American scholar, Bill Stonebarger, extended the evolution idea to explain societal transitions between ages. Few paid much attention until fifty years after his death in the early twenty-first century. Today his three books—*Twilight or Dawn: A Traveler's Guide to Free-Market Liberal Democracy, East Gilman Street,* and *Bill's Blogs*—are classics. All three are available in translation at most bookstores in Tanzania and Kenya and in the original English from the Internet giant Amazon.com.

Enlightenment; and (3) the economic power of diverse talents, free markets, free-trade—profit-making capitalism.

Today in Tanzania, as everywhere in the civilized world—including our colonies on the moon and Mars—we no longer need the fossil fuels that were so crucial to early progress. In sharp contrast to science-fiction fantasies of earlier times, people today all over the world enjoy lives not very different from middle-class families in the early Modern Age of the twenty-first century. We all enjoy today plentiful energy from nuclear plants, fission and fusion, supplemented by fossil fuels. In Africa we invented new tweaks in technology (notably in transportation, fabrics, and energy production), but otherwise there has not been that much change from twenty-first-century life in America, Europe, and some countries in Asia.

Correction—one big difference is that there are almost no poor people anywhere in the twenty-sixth century. In short, the dream pioneered in North America in 1776 has become reality in the twenty-sixth century—everyone on Earth now has *life, liberty, and pursuit of happiness* in abundance.

Paradoxically, the old Marxist claim, "From each according to his ability; to each according to his need," is now the rule rather than the exception. It was achieved not by government command and compulsion but by steady though slow worldwide growth in the three Modern Age essentials: (1) science and technology; (2) freedom of thought, especially freedom *from* religion (this took the longest to achieve); and (3) capitalist economics (diversity of talents, free markets, and free-trade profits).

We do have rich and poor inequality in the twenty-sixth century but not at the extremes of the early twenty-first century. More important, we no longer fear new technologies, growing populations, resource scarcity, or climate change. World population has been stable for centuries at about ten billion and most of those ten billion live long and comfortable middle-class lives.

We know now that the human hand and mind is the ultimate resource, and we no longer fear running out of other natural resources. World climate *has* warmed a degree or two in the past five hundred years, and for the most part, this has been beneficial.

The United States of North America can take justifiable pride in leading the way into the Modern Age in the first place. Tanzania takes pride in having added a fourth item to the trio of progress—a guaranteed national income (coming perhaps from our democratic tribal history). North America and Europe tried for years to soften unemployment, crime, indolence, and poverty by charitable welfare programs like food stamps, health care and education subsidies, minimum-wage laws, msximum sentences, unemployment insurance—and punishing prisons. People finally began to notice that these compassionate and punishing forms were not very effective and that only too often they increased dependency and crime. Prisons became so overcrowded everyone agreed that something had to be done.

Ever-increasing productivity, robots doing more and more in our homes and workplaces, growth in wealth, increasing efficiency, increased awareness of individual differences in talent, and growing unemployment made inevitable the idea of giving everyone a guaranteed minimum national income. This democratic way to redistribute wealth has diminished the dependency stigma and led to more rewarding and productive employment for the talented, more leisure for everyone, the encouragement of families, and a reduction in civic unrest and crime. We in Tanzania led the way. Most governments in the world followed by the end of the twenty-second century.

The Truth, the Whole Truth, and Nothing but the Truth

• • •

Aug. 18, 2004

> There was a young bard of Japan
> Whose limericks never would scan.
> When they said it was so,
> He replied, "Yes, I know,
> But I always try to fit as many syllables in the last line as I possibly can.

I ALSO TRY TO GET as many ideas in my weekly blogs as I possibly can. It can confuse. My son, Michael, liked a recent blog but suggested I simplify and devote a future one to my central point.

So here goes: the truth, the whole truth, and nothing but the truth.

Last week I wrote, "In my experience only a few experts in science or history have noticed the enormity of the changes brought on by modernity and how sharply they contrast with what came before. Even fewer have thought about what those big changes mean for today."

Although few people pay much attention to history, it is at the core of most political disputes today. I see four basic views:

1. Religious believers (by far the largest group in this country and this world) see history as an individual pilgrim's progress to a better (or worse) afterlife.

2. Progressives (the backbone and most popular of the nineteenth, twentieth and twenty-first centuries' secular clergy) see history as an ongoing struggle for justice between the haves and the have-nots.
3. Greens (the popular—often linked with the Progressive view in scientific, wealthy, and well-educated Western circles in the late twentieth and early twenty-first-century world) see it as *Homo sapiens* crowding out other species in an ever-more-destructive battle for the Earth's resources.
4. Evolution believers like me see human history in three evolving Ages—Hunting/Gathering to Agricultural to Modern.

The first three have basically no explanation for the astonishing explosion of worldwide wealth and population over the last two hundred years. They can only repeat the stories with modern twists: modern man turning *more* against God, modern haves taking *more* advantage of have-nots, and modern humans plundering nature *more* destructively.

These are intellectually stretching and, for the most part, are not even true. My evolution view is more likely.

In the glacially slow Hunting/Gathering Age, our *Homo sapiens* ancestors had to struggle with nature (and other species of the family *Homo*) to survive for more than a hundred thousand years. Most individuals lost the battle. Life for all was, as Thomas Hobbes wrote, "nasty, brutish, and short."

When humans learned to farm crops and to husband animals and then learned to read and write, populations soared, and chances for survival improved. We remember now the kings and queens; the lords, ladies, and the clergy; the rise and fall of many colorful and impressive civilizations on all continents; the courage of the elite warriors; the founding of many religions some of which still survive; and the moving music, art, and literature from all. We don't give much thought or credit though to the 99 percent who did the grunt work as merchants, craftsmen, peasants, serfs, or slaves. Their lives were still, for the most part, "nasty, brutish, and short."

Then came the Modern Age, born just a bit over two hundred years ago. It was founded not on history, religion, or ethnicity but on a new world of ideas. The new country in North America that founded it was the United States of America.

Humans in the United States of America, and soon in many other Western countries, found new ways to survive and prosper thanks to science and technology, freedom *of* and freedom *from* religion, and the power of free-market economics. Populations exploded, factories turned out millions of new products, and worldwide trade and travel increased exponentially. Peasants, serfs, and slaves disappeared—every person in the developed Western world could now command the energy equivalent of a hundred slaves. Even with the much greater numbers, most people in that modern world led lives that were increasingly rich, humane, and long. (And very recently many in the wanting-to-be-modern, developing non-Western world are catching on.)

All four views of history have consequences for believers and for society.

If you have the majority religious view in the Western world today, you will likely support measures to curb immoral behavior of individuals; measures to revere and reward traditional religions and individuals who practice those religions—Christian ones in the West, Muslim ones in the Middle East, and large sectiona of Asia and Africa, Hindu and Muslim ones in India, pagan and Confucian ones in China, and the like; measures to keep one religious group from attacking another; and charity to help the poor, homeless, disabled, and downtrodden. Sophisticated evangelical Christians may even support multiculturalism, and all religious people will work and pray to build a more peaceful and loving society. You would support these ideas unless you are a radical Muslim who still believes in jihad and forced conversion and defines morality in traditionally cruel ways detailed in Allah's words in holy books like the Quran. (Worthy of note: many Christians believed that same exclusive monotheistic idea five hundred years ago.)

If you are a Progressive, you will tend to look, as people did in Agricultural days, to the lords and ladies of government and academia (the modern clergy) for progress. You will probably support Occupy Wall Street and Black Lives Matter movements; minimum-wage laws to reduce inequality; laws to assure equal pay for women; laws to combat racism and sexism; laws to promote equal results as well as equal opportunities; laws to provide free health care and other *free* charitable government benefits; laws to restrict the marketplace; laws to increase taxes, especially on the wealthy; and, finally, you will be sympathetic to democratic socialism and devoted to social justice.

If you are a sustainable Green, you will look mainly to the local chiefs ("think global, act local") as people did in hunting-gathering days to control populations, technology, and wealth ("a growing economy means a shrinking ecosystem"); encourage an organic and natural back-to-Earth lifestyle; abandon fossil fuels; restrict or stop mining and drilling; control new technology; restrict travel; conserve resources; save endangered species; and, above all, combat climate change.

If you believe that history is evolving, and we are now just at the dawn of a Modern Age, you will support ways to increase worldwide freedom and wealth; reduce government regulation and dependency; support new developments in science and technology; encourage free enterprises, free markets, and free trades; advance freedom of religion and freedom *from* religion (especially in Muslim countries); and encourage and support diversity of talent in education and the marketplace. You will applaud developing countries getting rich now from new market economies, and you will treasure the Modern Age leadership of the United States.

There is overlap. Belief in one view does not mean necessary opposition to other views. The Progressive view, for example, does not rule out environmental protection, concern for climate change, or support for science and technology. It does rely on the government to do heavy pulling in these tasks. The religious view is pro-life and insists on personal, individual responsibility but does not rule out environmental protection. It does rely on the government to pass laws that punish sinners. The evolution view does not rule out pollution controls; aid for the poor, disabled, and immigrants; support for laws to curb prejudice and promote equal opportunity (though not equal results); universal health care; and cost-effective regulations for safety and the protection of the environment. It insists on freedom, less government, and more individual responsibility for progress.

The environmental view probably has the least overlap. In many ways it is flat-out opposed to the Modern Age (with an important exception for science and technology if Green enough). Fortunately, the environmental view is the least followed in practice. Most Greens today live rich, humane, and long lives in the upper-middle class of the United States or other developed countries. Cynics comment, "Everybody lies, but it doesn't matter since nobody pays attention." With Greens this translates to, "Everybody is for a lower carbon footprint, but it doesn't matter since nobody keeps score."

Thanksgiving through the Ages

• • •

Nov. 23, 2015

THANKSGIVING IS A UNIQUELY AMERICAN holiday. It is a good time to remember that the United States is an exceptional country. We launched the Modern Age.

When a family gets together for holiday dinner, someone is sure to suggest saying grace. When it comes my turn, I offer the following:

We humbly thank the farmers who grew the corn and fed the turkeys; the factory workers who made the tractors, trucks, computers, and silos; the truck drivers who transported the food; the grocery clerks, baggers, and stockers who sold it to us; the scientists and the companies who discovered and distributed better seed and better ways to protect the environment; the accountants who found ways to make it all more profitable; the bankers who lent the capital to buy the equipment, land, animals, and seeds; the miners, drillers, and fossil-fuel companies who provided the energy for the tractors, factories, and trucks; and the doctors, nurses, teachers, soldiers, police, and bureaucrats who healed, educated, and gave us security to achieve all of this—in short, all of the workers directly and indirectly responsible for our plentiful food, prosperity, freedom, and other blessings of the Modern Age.

Sun, water, carbon dioxide, and soil also played a part. If you believe an almighty God created them, you can thank Him or Her. For myself I think Gods or Goddesses nothing to do with it. Contrary to the Bible and the Quran (and most other religiously sacred books), my faith in that *Homo sapiens* has had a long and natural evolution. We inherited both our genes and memes from generations past. So, too, there has been a natural evolution of societies.

There was a Hunting/Gathering Age of more than one hundred thousand years, when people lived in tribes; private property did not exist; violence was common; life was hard; good hunting/gathering lands were critical; our remote ancestors competed with carnivores (and other *Homo* species!); and with nature itself for survival. Adventure and leisure were common, but the average human lived only twenty-five years or so.

An Agricultural Age of ten thousand years, when cities and civilizations came to be; populations and food production exploded; wealth was land, gold, and slaves; wars and violence were nearly constant; religions arose whose clergy set the moral patterns, tone and agendas (memes); inequality was the norm; slaves, serfs, and peasants worked and suffered in poverty while lords, ladies, and clergy ruled in extravagance; average life-spans increased ten years or so.

The Modern Age began in 1776 in the United States and is now only a little more than two hundred years old; science and technology created with the help of capitalism and freedom of and from religion provided wealth and resources in abundance; populations exploded, again; slavery, serfdom, and peasantry disappeared; democracy became common; exclusive monotheistic religion declined but did not disappear; wars and personal violence declined but did not disappear; average life-spans for all increased by forty years or more.

How does this view of Evolution in human history view help with current problems?

CLIMATE CHANGE

The climate has changed often in past ages. No doubt it will change in future ones. Left-liberal Progressive leaders like Paul Krugman, the Nobel Prize-winning economist and *New York Times* columnist, claims, "When President Obama describes climate change as the greatest threat we face, he's exactly right. Terrorism can't and won't destroy our civilization; but global warming could and might."

Krugman and Obama may be right about terrorism but are shockingly wrong about climate change. The idea that one or two degrees of warming or cooling (even partisans admit that is what we can expect from our best international efforts to reduce carbon pollution) will destroy our civilization is so at odds with human experience over past millennia and indeed so ludicrous that I am shocked so many educated and intelligent people take it seriously.

If you substitute *overpopulation, resource scarcity, nuclear accidents,* or *DDT* for *global warming* in the quote in the previous paragraph, you can see where the threat is coming from—modern clergy scientist advisers like John Holdren, James Hansen, Paul Ehrlich, and the late Carl Sagan and Rachel Carson. All are fine scientists in their fields, with good intentions and high intelligence, but with embarrassingly low predictive batting averages for predictions.

Racism

The Modern Age has already abolished slavery, serfdom, and peasantry. It is on its way to abolish poverty. But it can never repeal the natural bell curves of life that make for diversity. Recent attempts to do so have routinely led to disaster—the Holocaust; Soviet slave labor camps; and the acute shortage of wealth, resources, and immigrants along with increases in violence and sharp deceases in wealth in Cuba, North Korea, Venezuela, and other countries still enamored by socialism/communism. Even laudable, well-intentioned attempts in the West with government-led social-justice programs designed to mandate equality often backfire and lead to family breakdown, dependency, crime, overflowing prisons, and drug and violence problems in major cities. Current well-intentioned ideas in this country like white privilege, equal outcomes, wealth inequality, and multiculturalism ignore the diversity of evolution and can lead to tragedy if pursued widely and deeply enough. Our challenge today is to invent new ways of living with inequality and diversity—providing income and dignity to the less talented and avoiding the crippling power of victimhood and dependency.

Terrorism

This is a toughie. In medieval times, Islam was a world leader in science, health, education, and scholarly achievement. Despite its early schism into Shiite and Sunni, Islam never had a full-fledged Renaissance, Reformation, or Enlightenment as Christianity did hundreds of years ago (in a chaos of bloody wars). As a result, Islam today is grossly inferior to the West in its treatment of women, its lack of freedom for and from religions, and its contempt for basic civil rights. Whether we can help or hinder the chance for Islam to enter the Modern Age is problematic. For starters, we need to admit the religious nature of the conflict. Accepting unlimited Muslim refugees is a serious issue, especially in Europe. How best to use our superior military power is another problematic issue. Suicidal terrorism is a weapon of the weak. But if it succeeds, as it sometimes does, it can also strike suicidal fear in the strong. I am like most people today. I frankly don't know what we can do. The best advice may be simply a mix of caution, courage, and not giving in to fear.

In the long run, I predict the Modern Age will triumph.

The Itsy-Bitsy Spider and Passwords

● ● ●

MARCH 7, 2016

IN MY OLD AGE, I find myself more impressed with the wisdom locked in children's songs.

> The itsy-bitsy spider crawled up a waterspout
> Down came the rain and washed the spider out
> Out came the sun and dried up all the rain
> The itsy-bitsy spider crawled up the spout again.

The spider is like the mythical Sisyphus, condemned by the gods to push a large boulder up a hill on to watch it roll back down and then to repeat this for all eternity. It's an image made to order for existentialists.

I empathize with both the spider and Sisyphus after struggling with my computer. Again.

When I was a kid, a password was something you had to remember to be a part of the gang. It's not much different today with the computer gang and the smartphone gang (I don't have a smartphone, so I'm not that sure here). In any case, it sure gets more complicated.

Recently I had to change my printer. The old one was printing a lot of unasked for *zzzzzzzzzzzzz*'s. As all of you know only too well, whenever you change anything on a computer, you are in for a lot of *zzzzzzzzzzzzz*'s. Wouldn't you know, along with installing the new printer, I had to update the operating system on my iMac. I did.

Why, oh why, do they also change the names of some of my favorite applications when you update? "Address Book" served me well. Why change it to "Contacts"—not even on the same alphabetic shelf? I admit this is an old man's complaint. I even complain when friends, family, or senior "helpers" change the exact spot in my kitchen where my morning cereal or doughnuts or coffee are stored.

That operating-system update also meant I had to get an updated version of some key programs I use often. That cost money. But I paid and did it. The OS update also meant remembering and redoing many user IDs and passwords to sites I use often on the Internet. It also mysteriously enough messed up my e-mail program. Undoing all the damage the changes caused was hard, but I managed this, too—with the help of a few hundreds of dollars' worth of guru coaching from a friendly and knowledgeable Mac guy.

Like the itsy-bitsy spider, I did manage to crawl up the spout. Like Sisyphus, to roll that boulder up the hill—to write and send out this blog.

And then I had to groan when I read stories about Apple's fight with the government about cracking the iPhone security system. Last year I wrote a blog about that computer cloud. Perhaps it is related to the *noosphere*, the place once proposed by a Belgian philosopher and Jesuit priest, Pierre Teilhard de Chardin, where conscious intelligence resides. Chardin thought the ultimate destiny of humankind was literally to evolve into the noosphere, which he identified also as a reunion with the body of Christ! Perhaps in my advanced age, that is what I am doing now.

I do believe that the noosphere of Chardin has a lot in common with the modern "computer cloud" that Apple, IBM, and many other companies and individuals use to store and process information. The truth is that I don't have a very clear understanding of either.

This computer cloud is apparently where iPhone users like the San Bernardino terrorists and New York drug dealers stored their encrypted passwords and phone messages that the FBI now wants to see. Apple argues that they can't compromise the security of all its iPhone customers, even for the sake of national security.

I think this is tempest in a teapot. I have enough trouble with my own user IDs and passwords to worry about national security in the cloud noosphere. Seriously, I'm sure Apple, the world's wealthiest company, could afford a few dollars of their software engineer's time to break into the cloud and let the FBI get a peek at the terrorists' or the drug dealers' contacts, passwords, and messages. AT&T and local telephone companies routinely obey judge's orders to wiretap telephones of suspected criminals. What makes the iPhone so special?

I should note that this morning, the *Wall Street Journal* had an editorial taking the side of Apple in the controversy. The column's main point seems to be that in recent court rulings, the government was using a law passed two hundred years ago!

So? The Constitution was also ratified two hundred years ago and is still serviceable. At least the late Justice Scalia thought it was. Obama may have a different opinion. I usually agree with the *WSJ* editorials. This time I did not.

The truth is that I realize thT I am seriously over my head here and in danger of drowning. I suspect most reporters and editorial pundits are in danger, too. For instance can any make much sense of this sentence in the *WSJ* last Wednesday? Mr. Comey, the FBI director, said, "There was a mistake made in that 24 hours after the attack when the county at the FBI's request took steps that made it impossible later to cause the phone to back up to the iCloud." Umm.

The Cloud and the Noosphere

● ● ●

Jan. 6, 2014

THE CLOUD IS A MYSTERIOUS closet somewhere out there where the Internet, mobile phone messages, Tweets, credit card numbers, Snowden's purloined NSA documents, miscellaneous computer files, and heaven only knows what else are stored.

Perhaps it is related to the noosphere a place once proposed by a Belgian philosopher and Jesuit priest, Pierre Teilhard de Chardin, where conscious intelligence hides. Chardin thought the ultimate destiny of humankind was to evolve into the noosphere, which he identified as a reunion with the body of Christ.

On a more earthly plane, the Harvard scholar Steven Pinker in a new book, *The Better Angels of Our Nature: Why Violence Has Declined*, attributes the decline of violence in recent years to the noosphere (I don't know that Pinker used that word). Actually, Pinker points to specific parts of the noosphere (I call them *memes*) that he claims are responsible for that decline—trade and rational thought. The virtues of trade are well known. The virtues of rational thought are not. Following the lead of Teilhard de Chardin, Pinker, and with a nod to the Princeton psychologist Julian Jaynes (*The Origin of Consciousness in the Breakdown of the Bicameral Mind*), here is my hypothesis.

There is a geosphere (rocks, air, and water), a biosphere (living things), and a noosphere (a world of conscious thought). All three change over time. In the distant past, the geosphere—atoms and radiation—was all there was. When life came along, a billion or so years ago, genes were top dogs. When human life became conscious, three of four thousands of years ago, the noosphere began to slowly grow, and memes took charge.

Today, with the sudden spurt of growth that comes with this mysterious computer cloud, we may be getting close to...?

We can't really know, but for sure the world's geosphere and biosphere are being shaped now by memes of the noosphere. This noosphere is turning slowly away from traditional zero-sum hunting/gathering and agricultural memes and more and more in the direction of rational scientific ones.

The actual noosphere today is like the atmosphere—and just as changeable and controversial. You breathe it into your meme-choked mind just as you breathe air into your lungs. If you live in a college town, as I do—or on the East or West Coast—you can't help but *breathe in* a distinctly Progressive and Green noosphere, which has its virtues, but also its faults.

Among the many virtues are increasing tolerances for different lifestyles, different racial and ethnic groups, different sexual choices, and different thought patterns (this latter with severe limits). This all-pervading Progressive and Green noosphere also values rational thought and science (again with limits) and prefers nonviolent solutions. It has unlimited empathy for the poor, the underdog, and the downtrodden and a passionate interest in the environment (in theory).

These pluses come with some serious minuses.

This progressive noosphere puts sincerity and good intentions above results. At present, it is close to paralyzed by the supposed evils of inequality and lack of sustainability. Insofar as the Progressive preference for Green and sustainable leads to more efficiency, it is a plus. Like traditional free-market capitalism *Light Green* offers hope. Getting more efficiency is the best—in fact, the only—way to make profits, to grow economies, and to amass wealth.

Alas, the Progressive noosphere veers only too often into what I call *Dark Green* territory, where growing the economy means shrinking the ecosystem. If fear of inequality doesn't do it first, Dark Green threatens to destroy the Modern Age.

Besides leaning to the Green and sustainable, the Progressive noosphere also leans antibusiness and—although I hesitate to say it—anti-American. As such, it seeps willy-nilly into our collective unconscious and shakes our national confidence. It whispers (often shouts) that the United States is not that great. In fact at its worst it claims that our Western civilization, led by the United States, is responsible for raping and pillaging poor societies of Asia, Africa, and Native America. If they fight back now, we have it coming. (Popular reaction to this view may be partially at least responsible for the recent popularity of billionaire Donald Trump.)

The Green part of the Progressive noosphere has dogmas, also demonstrably false but fervently believed as though they came from a religious bible: (1) the world is vastly overpopulated; (2) resources are running out; (3) pollution is getting worse; and (4) one particular pollutant, carbon, is now said to cause global warming (climate change) and will end up destroying us.

The left-liberal part of the Progressive noosphere also has anti-American axioms, demonstrably false but fervently believed as though they came from a religious bible: (1) Westerners got their wealth and dominance by robbing others (or by raping the Earth itself in the Green version); (2) Wall Street, and capitalists in general, are greedy vultures preying on 99 percent of the people with excessive profits stolen from the people; (3) we should follow the lead of Europe in promoting more socialism and less cowboy capitalism; (4) there is nothing superior about our Western culture, and we should humbly admit that we are just one among many civilizations (multiculturalism), some of which may well be superior (even the primitive Hunting/Gathering cultures of Africa, Native America, and Asia); and (5) democracy means equality, so we should strive for equal outcomes as well as equal treatment under the laws.

Some contrarians today like me strongly disagree with these axioms, just as some disagreed with fellow travelers about communism. Fellow travelers were popular in the Great Depression and, in muted form, continued to be popular through the late twentieth century right up to the collapse of the Soviet Empire. Ronald Reagan sided with the contrarians when he said prophetically, "I believe that communism is a sad, bizarre chapter in human history whose last pages are even now being written." And so it came to pass.

Let us hope the same will come to pass with the Progressive Green noosphere now so firmly entrenched on college campuses and in both the East and West Coast literati.

Intermission

• • •

I WENT TO THE BANK one April morning to make a deposit and came upon the Madison Farmer's Market and the annual running of the Crazy Legs eight-kilometer race. I ran in this race twenty or so years ago. Now I am in my nineties, and walking a block is all I can manage. Even that is difficult.

Madison is supposed to be a socially conscious, kindly, and warm-hearted city. Recently, racial gaps are making the news in my city. The Madison public schools have nearly half nonwhite minority students, and there is already evidence of white flight. As liberals hasten to point out, there is a substantial gap between the scores of minorities and whites on achievement tests. The liberal people of Madison expect equal results when we offer equal opportunity.

This gorgeous spring morning, the sun is out and bright, and more than fifteen thousand runners have signed up (at a stiff forty-dollar fee) to run from Capitol Square to the football stadium at Camp Randall (named for a Civil War army encampment that freed the slaves). I could, but won't, count on the fingers of one hand the number of black or other nonwhite minority adults I see among the runners. Is that because of the stiff fee or a simple lack of interest in a white-majority event?

I love writing blogs. When I begin writing, I never know how it will go or how it will end. When you get as old as I am, you lose the ability to get much pleasure from playing sports, travel (even walking), sex, and so many other things. I am grateful I can still enjoy wrestling with ideas. The examples that follow may damn me as a hopeless old fogey (and a racist bigot besides). I'll take the chance.

The Stockholm syndrome

• • •

June 30, 2014

THE STOCKHOLM SYNDROME IS WHEN captives identify with their captors—the oppressed with the oppressors. We have a striking example today in Western countries, where many in the middle and upper classes (which some leftist intellectuals view as the *oppressors*) are adopting the culture of the underclass (which the same leftist intellectuals view as the *oppressed*).

We in this country are trying so hard to be fair, generous, and accommodating (patronizing?) to diverse nonwhite minorities today that we may be in danger of losing our exceptional character as the country that has offered, and still does, freedom and opportunity to all. In short, we may be harming the people we want to help by making and keeping them dependent: by destroying their families; their self-respect; and any wealth they might have made by working to help themselves.

When Jefferson wrote, "all men are created equal and endowed by their Creator with certain unalienable Rights, that among these are Life, Liberty and the Pursuit of Happiness," he meant equality under the law—free *citizens*, not *subjects* of an oppressive government. Jefferson was aware that people could never be equally gifted, equally wealthy, equally honored, or that we could all could work equally hard with equal success. I doubt that he could foresee that equality and the pursuit of happiness might lead to an obese, pregnant, unwed mother with four children in tow (all with different, long-gone fathers), tattoos covering her body, and rings in her nose and tongue, sneering to her social workers, "Fuck you, nigga."

Please don't assume that either the welfare woman or the social workers in my example are black or white. In our dumbed-down current culture, elite and not-so-elite citizens can't seem to get enough of underclass culture. Thugs become heroes. Sex is rape. Music, movies, cable TV, and ordinary people use language that would make a sailor blush (noting the first title of this book I'm not excusing myself). Pornography is number one on the Internet. Unwed mothers move from disgrace to acceptance to desirability while fathers disappear—often to jail. Tattoos and piercings in noses, navels, lips, tongues, and genitals are becoming as common as dirt.

Breaking news: heavily tattooed cameramen from a new company, Vice Media, accompanied a heavily tattooed Dennis Rodman on his trip to North Korea to play basketball with his buddy, the dictator Kim Jong-un (who so far as I know is free of tattoos). Video clips from this trip and others like it have become so popular they have made Vice Media very valuable. Media giants like Disney, Time Warner, NBC, and Fox News are battling to buy it for billions of dollars.

More breaking news: I was taught never to use the N-word, but according to *Capitol Times* (Madison's Progressive newspaper), the use of *nigga* is so common now among young blacks, it has spread to young middle-class and upper-class whites in our otherwise politically correct high schools.

Progressive zealots make a fuss over the Cleveland Indians, the Washington Redskins, the mildly racist comments of an NBA team owner, or any and all opposition to gay marriage, abortion, or feminist dogma. But they don't bat an eyelid when rap artists, movie producers, or video-game designers popularize misogyny, violence, and vulgarity. The F-word is so common now it barely raises an eyebrow. Even a quality movie like *Saving Private Ryan* or *Apocalypse Now* has soldiers using language I rarely heard in my days in boot camp and on navy ships and bases during World War II. My mother would have washed their mouths out with soap.

Here are some examples from the popular and wealthy rap singer and music promoter and executive, Dr. Dre. (*Rolling Stone* magazine ranks him as fifty-sixth on their list of one hundred greatest artists of all time. *Forbes* estimated his net worth as $550 million.)

> Yeah, that's what the fuck I'm talkin' about,
> We have your motherfuckin' record company surrounded,
> Put down the candy and let the little boy go,
> You knowhatI'msayin, punk motherfucker.

Or...

> Bitches ain't shit but hoes and tricks,
> Lick on these nuts and suck the dick,
> Get the fuck out after you're done.

Or Eminem, the popular and rich white rapper:

> Eninem, Wonder Boy, Shady,
> Its' goin' down baby.
> Ayo, Em, I got you back my nigga
>
> Damn right I said my nigga,
> That's my nigga,
> Tricky
>
> Extra-terrestrial, killing pedestrians,
> Raping lesbians while they're screaming,
> "Let's just be friends!"

> Can't think of a better way to define poetic justice,
> Can I hold grudges, mind saying, "Let it go, fuck this."
> Heart's saying, "I will, once I bury this bitch alive,
> Hide the shovel and then drive off into the sunset."

There may be some gut-wrenching honesty in Dr. Dre's and Eminem's lyrics, but that is not much of an excuse. I hasten to admit, too, that I have enjoyed movies that use vulgarity but are more subtle and interesting than the Hayes-censored movies of my youth. And finally, I admit to hoping my previous title, *Bill's Fuckin' Blogs*, makes me rich and famous.

But still. Is it all that great to call women whores and bitches? Is it really OK to make violence a romantic, common, and fun thing? Is it that great to have children out of wedlock or destroy families and lead young men into drugs, crime, and prison? Is it really that attractive to have tattoos cover bodies, color hair green, and have metal rings and spikes adorn noses, tongues, lips, and genitalia—all presumably in search of some kind of primitive charm?

Is the N-word OK now? Is it OK to use the F-word in every sentence? And finally, is it good to encourage us all to hate the productive rich and imitate the unproductive and dependent lower class in lifestyles, as so many movies and television shows do nowadays? (Note to young readers: in the Great Depression of the 1930s, movies often idolized the rich.)

I'll answer my own questions. No, I don't think it is OK. I think it is depressing—and in major part, disgusting.

The Bell Curve

• • •

April 14, 2014

The Bell Curve: Intelligence and Class Structure in American Life is a controversial best-selling book, published in 1994 and written by Harvard psychologist Richard J. Herrnstein (who died before the book was released) and libertarian political scientist Charles Murray. Their book caused a near earthquake in academia. Many left-liberal professors called it racist slime. Some vowed to never read it and advised their students to do likewise. The clergy ignored it.

The sober book's message is hard to ignore: intelligence is important, IQ tests reliably measure it, and bell curves of the results challenge the Progressive view that we should have equal outcomes as well as equal opportunities.

Our country is dedicated to the principle that all should be given an equal chance to life, liberty, and the pursuit of happiness.

Our founders meant equality under the law. They knew that people were unique and unequal in all physical, mental, and emotional traits. In fact, we are all without exception unequal in many traits: intelligence, health, speed, athleticism, wealth, status, GPAs, winning average in sports, test scores, many personality traits, and so on. Unless you impose totalitarian controls, you will never get pure equality in any society of human beings. And even then, there will be diversity in victims. Not the trials of Cuba, North Korea and all the Soviet bloc countries including the Soviet Union itself.

Herrnstein and Murray point out that there is in nature a bell curve for all physical and mental traits of humans and, for that matter, for all living things. All of these physical and mental abilities are grounded in a combination of genes and environment (and, more controversially, in free choices). Teasing out the respective contributions of genetic, environmental, and free choice causes is difficult and probably a fool's errand. Regardless of how they get there, most living things—plant, animal, and human—fall in the middle of bell-shaped curves for traits, with a few at the high end and a few at the low end.

For instance, most men are between five feet seven and six feet one in height. A few reach a height of six feet eight or even seven feet, and a few are very short, below five feet two. Women have a slightly different bell curve for height where the median is shorter. There is overlap of course. A very few women do reach seven feet, and very few men are shorter than five feet two.

If you do a bell curve of punctuality, most people will be in the middle, rarely more than ten minutes late or ten minutes early. A few will consistently be more than a half hour late, and a few will consistently be half an hour early. Again, there will be overlap. In addition, some typically late people will occasionally come early, and some typically early people will occasionally come late.

It is the same with all human traits and talents— intelligence, height, weight, courage, kindness, friendliness, leadership, strength, quickness, speed, sense of humor, musical ability, mathematical ability, verbal facility, sales ability, street smarts, determination, patience, aggressiveness, athleticism, meanness, veracity, shyness, extroversion, perseverance, disease susceptibilities, and so on. Most of us are in the middle range with a few at each end of a bell-shaped curve.

If you want to play in the NBA, NFL, or NHL, you will need a rare combination of traits at the extreme upper end of the bell curves that measure some of these traits and talents. If you want to win a Nobel Prize, become president, be a CEO of a large corporation or be a professor at Harvard, you will need a different but equally rare combination at the extreme upper end of the bell curves that measure some of these traits and talents.

In all cases, you will also need some money, family support, a lot of aggressive energy, and a bit of luck.

Now we come to the controversial part. Some *roughly* definable subsets of human beings have different averages on some human traits—different medians, different averages, and different extremes.

Males and females, for instance, have different means and extremes on most meaures. Females seldom compete with males in sports and endeavors that demand strength and speed. African American men dominate professional basketball, football, and track, but there are also many top white players. Jewish and Asian men and women dominate Nobel and Pulitzer Prize winners, PhD degrees in the sciences and arts. They tend to get the top jobs in industries and government posts, but there are also many non-Jewish and non-Asian winners.

Here is the critical point. Whites, Blacks, Jews, Germans, Irish, Africans, Asians, Native Americans, Hispanic Americans, Asian Americans, rich and poor people of all colors, religions, and sexes—and remember please all these are all only very *roughly* definable groups. In other words, all groups are made up of a broad range of unique individuals, a few scoring at the upper end of the bell curves and a few at the lower end for many traits. This means it makes no sense define, publicize, deprecate, punish, patronize, or take pride in membership in any of these roughly definable groups. All of us are individuals. There is only one human race today—only one *Homo sapiens*.

Worth noting is that today almost everyone in the world today is a "mixed race." Our President Obama is not black, he is half Irish as well as half black. He is not unusual. We all share many genes and many environments. Even male and female may not be mutually exclusive groups as the LGBT community is reminding us today.

Despite all these facts, you yourself are a unique mixture of genes, environments, and choices. When others want to define and limit you to any average group trait, they take away your unique individuality and punish, patronize, or praise you without regard to where you personally fit on all those bell curves of height, weight, courage, kindness, friendliness, leadership, intelligence, health, strength, quickness, speed, sense of humor, musical ability, mathematical ability, verbal ability, determination, patience, aggressiveness, athleticism, meanness, veracity, shyness, extroversion, street smarts, perseverance, disease susceptibilities, and so forth.

There is only one human race, *Homo sapiens*. Racial prejudice—or prejudice against any human group—is a sign of ignorance and moral stupidity and is always bad.

Educators as well as all people would do well to follow the dancer Martha Graham's advice: "There is a vitality, a life force, an energy, a quickening, that is translated through you into action, and because there is only one of you in all time, this expression is unique. If you block it, it will never exist in any other medium. The world will not have it."[3]

That said, intellectual leaders, educators, politicians, and journalists who insist on defining and publicizing so-called racial differences in education, wealth, socioeconomic status, and the like are themselves the real *racists*. We all would be wise to follow Martin Luther King Jr., who preached the virtues of an individual- oriented color-blind society, even for those with perfectly normal eyesight: "I have a dream that my four little children will one day live in a nation where they will not be judged by the color of their skin but by the content of their character."

---

3 *The Life and Work of Martha Graham* (1991), p. 264.

Inequality

● ● ●

Sept. 14, 2015

When I was young, I played a fair amount of basketball, football, and golf. I was no LeBron James, Aaron Rodgers, or Tiger Woods, though. I was slow in speed and on the low end of bell curve in strength. The awful truth is, I did not have enough athletic talent, courage, aggressiveness, perseverance, hard work, or whatever bell-curve traits it takes to make the varsity teams in high school, much less in college. Stars on the gridiron, the basketball floor, or the golf course got dates with the prettiest girls and got the most acclaim from peers, parents, and the public. I was and still am sorry for my shortcomings in sports. I am forced now to mostly be a fan but not a jock.

Some men like Ben Carson, Bernie Sanders, Donald Trump, Bill Clinton, or Barack Obama could succeed in many areas, but I could not. Academics, though, were duck soup for me. I routinely aced tests, made honor rolls, and ended up class valedictorian. This pleased my parents and some of the public but did not do much for my peer popularity. I was high on the bell curve for academics but low on the bell curve for sports. I was also no doubt low on the bell curve for many other traits and talents and average or high on the bell curves for still other traits and talents. In other words, In short I was and I am boringly and shockingly normal.

Bell curves are not popular with movers and shakers today. Our Founding Fathers committed us to an equality ethic that often conflicts with the harsh facts of nature's inequality. Thomas Jefferson wrote, "We hold these truths to be self-evident, that all men are created equal, that they are endowed by their Creator with certain unalienable Rights, that among these are Life, Liberty and the Pursuit of Happiness."

Jefferson was enough of a realist to realize equality had severe limits. The Declaration promised equal treatment under the law but did not imply the absurd view that human beings were equal in all traits and talents or we could expect or promise equal results.

For instance, women in most sports seldom compete with men and for good reason. They have average bell-curve scores considerably less than men for strength, endurance, speed, quickness, and athleticism.

This in no way means women are inferior to men. We prize achievement at the upper ends of the bell curve in both sports and academics—maybe more than we should—but sports *and* academics barely scratch the surface of human traits and talents. LeBron James, Aaron Rodgers, Tiger Woods—as well as the top scientists, scholars, and writers—do collect the most money, the top jobs, and the most prizes. They are plainly more talented and certainly on the upper levels of the bell curves for traits needed—in their fields. They probably also work harder. Working hard is still another talent!

Despite these stubborn facts, some cling to the view that equal opportunity is fine, but we should also strive for and expect equal outcomes for groups. This view is especially damaging in education. Educators routinely face a difficult choice. On the one hand, you want to hold your students to high expectations. On the other hand, you don't want to hold them to expectations you know they are incapable of achieving. Teachers, principals, and superintendents often have to shoulder the blame when their student's score on the low end of academic tests graded on a bell curve. Jeepers! This is grossly unfair. Never mentioned is the possibility their students might simply have less talent for academics. Maybe they also have less talent for hard work or some other needed trait. Whether this is due to genes or environment doesn't much matter. It is what it is.

In a free trade, it's true that all parties are winners if the trade is fair. But winning does not necessarily translate to equal wealth, equal fame, or equal happiness. I consider myself a winner in Life, Liberty, and the Pursuit of Happiness race. But I don't come close to the wealth and fame of sports stars and pop music celebrities—or Nobel Prize winners.

When black activists today claim "black lives matter," they point to an obvious moral truth. Unfortunately, racism does exist, and the police are clearly unjustified in racially profiling any citizen. But they sometimes do. Blacks should not profile the police. But they sometimes do. In numbers, far more blacks are killed in black-on-black encounters than in black-on-police encounters. The obvious point is that the black community needs more, not less, police and that we *all* deserve to matter. We *all* deserve opportunity.

I even think we have enough wealth in this country that we *all* deserve a decent standard of living. But expecting *equal* outcomes is like me expecting to play quarterback for the Green Bay Packers or forward for the Cleveland Cavaliers—and making the money these stars do.

Inequality comes with freedom. Countries like Cuba, North Korea, and the former Mao's China and Stalin's Soviet Union sacrificed freedom for equal outcomes. They got police states, slave labor camps, and shortages of nearly everything instead. Better to learn to live with inequality.

Nature gives clues.

There are three trillion trees in the world according to the Yale School of Forestry and Environmental Studies—that's 442 trees for each person on Earth. There are around ten thousand different tree species. One of those species is the sugar maple (*Acer saccharum*).

A friend of ours runs a family sugar bush in Vermont. She makes quite a few gallons of maple syrup every winter using Acer saccarum. Another friend makes maple syrup in Wisconsin, where the trees are also Acer saccarum. But they may or may not be as productive. The environment makes a difference. Individual maple tree bell curves do, too. Some Acer saccarum maple trees yield a lot of sap, and some yield less.

Some sap is sweeter than others. Most are in the middle range. The end result is that Vermont maple syrup is not that different from Wisconsin maple syrup or maple syrup from Michigan or New York or wherever.

That is the way nature works—a few at each end and most in the middle. You end up with bell-curve distributions in all species of trees, ants, corn, cows, roses, and all living plants and animals. In addition, and not surprisingly, you also have different bell curves for the same species in different environments. It's not a simple matter of genes. Nor is it a simple matter of environment. It's always a combination. And for humans, I think free choice and effort also make a contribution. The beauty of diversity!

Nature (genes *and* environment) cares for the middle. There is little room for blame or praise. In the case of humans, religious and political philosophies tell us that we *should* be sympathetic with individuals and groups at both ends of the bell curve. In the normal course of events, we don't need to worry much about those at the talented ends—LeBron James, Aaron Rodgers, Tiger Woods, Albert Einstein, Beyoncé Knowles-Carter, Donald Trump, the Koch brothers, George Soros, and Barack Obama can manage on their own. People at the less talented ends, though, may need help. What kind, though?

In Western countries influenced by Christianity, the most common help given is need-based charity—food stamps, housing subsidies, aid to dependent families, health care, housing and education subsidies, and the like. This kind of charitable help was cimmon in most Agricultural Age civilizations. It was especially common in Christian ones, but all religious groups have practiced charity. As the Modern Age has become progressively more technical and sophisticated, opportunities at the lower ends of human bell curves keep diminishing, and it becomes unrealistic to expect success in the free marketplace. This is also fast becoming true of many traditional middle class jobs. These harsh facts seem to increase the need for more charity as the Progressive clergy typically propose. The charitable approach, however, often leads to dependent victimhood and from there to drugs, crime, misery, and prison.

An alternative might be a minimum national income—for instance, social security checks for all not just the retired or disabled. All of us are handicapped in some way. Rue, this would still leave citizens dependent on government redistribution. But as with seniors and disabled today, it would take much of the sting out of the dependence. Cash charity for all instead of the need-based variety for victims would encourage family bonds and discourage drugs and crime. How many social security recipients do you know who are homeless or in prison for drugs, looting, or killing people?

For details on one cash approach, I recommend the book of libertarian political scientist Charles Murray, *In Our Hands: A Way to Replace the Welfare State*.

At least one of our Founding Fathers, Thomas Paine, favored a scheme like this. He wanted to give every citizen a check for a thousand dollars on their twenty-first birthday!

Sustainability in Education

● ● ●

Oct. 19, 2015

THE EDUCATIONAL ESTABLISHMENT (WHICH I sometimes label a monastic order of the modern clergy) is close to unanimous in its dedication to the sustainable and the diverse.

My alma mater, Antioch, boasts on its website that the college...

> takes its commitments to diversity and sustainability seriously. Projects like the 5-acre solar field built this fall support the College's goal of heating and cooling the entire campus solely with renewable geothermal and solar energy by 2016. This and other initiatives are part of a larger plan to be one of the most sustainable schools in the nation. The College also stewards the 1,000-acre nature preserve that surrounds the campus, and many students make the farm-to-table connection at the Antioch Farm, which grows food served in the dining halls.

Antioch has always been a leader in diversity, too. When I went there in the late forties, it was among the few colleges that admitted blacks. One of my friends and fellow students was Coretta Scott, later to marry Martin Luther King Jr. and lead civil rights marches. Another was Leon Higginbotham Jr., who became the first black man appointed to a Federal Appeals Court. Later, in the late 1960s, Antioch was again a pioneer in recruiting inner-city poor blacks with poor credentials for a college education. In this case Antioch was not as successful in graduation rates or in students' achievements later in their lives.

These twin demands for more diversity and more sustainability account for much of the huge increases in cost for a college education today.

Part of it is simple supply and demand. A century ago, only one out of three hundred adults had a college education. Harvard tuition in 1915 was $150 ($3,303 in today's dollars). Today nearly half of high-school grads aim for college once they learn that a college graduate gets better jobs and earns more money. Colleges have expanded but not enough to take care of the increased demand.

More students, along with more diversity and with fewer college slots, lead to higher cost per student. The cost of living has increased 2,263 percent since 1915; college tuition has increased more than 40,000 percent. Alas, many graduates, especially those majoring in liberal arts and social sciences, humanities, or environmental studies, end up waiting tables or clerking at Wal-Mart and having trouble paying back their student loans.

You add still more cost when you demand a more sustainable campus to: power college operations on solar, wind, and geothermal energy; create new courses in sustainable science and redo courses to add sustainable content; subsidize public transportation; upgrade buildings and infrastructures; install low-flow showers and toilets; recycle all trash; restrict parking spaces; wash dishes and dining utensils instead of using plastic disposables; and serve organic food, preferably grown within twenty-five miles of campus (farm-to-table from the Antioch Farm).

The conservative National Association of Scholars (NAS) gives a lowball estimate of the cost of sustainability in higher education of $3.4 billion a year.

To carry the Green and Progressive crusade beyond the campus, the Progressive-Green clergy urges graduates to live simpler lives; "significantly limit their consumption"; keep a low carbon footprint; buy carbon offsets to atone for business and pleasure air flights; give up bottled water and plastic bags; repair, recycle, and reuse rather than buy new; "Save the Earth, don't give birth"; "Wrap with care, save the polar bear"; and most important, never forget that a growing economy means a shrinking ecosystem. Do all this as Pope Francis advises, to help the poor and save the Earth.

It is noteworthy that the modern Progressive-Green clergy itself manages to dodge most of its own advice—as did many of the Christian clergy in medieval times and continues to do so today. Professor's salaries have also increased considerably as hours in the classroom have decreased dramatically. (To give Pope Francis credit, he does seem to favor the simple and humble lifestyle for himself.)

This all points to a fatal flaw in sustainability and diversity dogma—it is built on an Agricultural Age belief that wealth and resources are severely limited, that the Earth's resources and therefore the world's wealth are like a big pie. If someone gets a bigger piece, others will have to make do with smaller pieces. This actually was true in both the Agricultural Age and in the Hunting/Gathering Age, when nations, tribes, and individuals fought fiercely and endlessly over land, gold, slaves—or in the earlier Age over gold and good hunting-and-gathering land. The violence and wars were so fierce and bloody because land, gold, slaves, and good hunting-and-gathering land were always in short supply.

If resources for wealth were that limited now, how could China, with the largest population in the world, have reduced poverty so much that it has risen to be number two in world wealth. And it has done this when the rest of the world was also getting richer, populations everywhere were exploding, and people everywhere were using more of the presumed scarce resources?

How did China do it? The same way we did. They abandoned state control and went to an essential of the Modern Age, a market/capitalist economy. The Modern Age by now has proved conclusively—first in the United States, later in Europe, and still later in most of the developing world—that wealth is not a fixed quantity. The whole world in the Modern Age is much much richer in every way than the same whole world was in all earlier Ages. Wealth grows when we make more efficient use of resources, when we do more with less. In short, wealth grows from smart work, free trade, and healthy profits—in a word, capitalism.

I know, I know. The modern surge for sustainability is designed not to make us rich; it is supposed to save us from climate-change disasters. (Forty years ago some of the same clergy were preaching to save us from population "bombs" and resource scarcity.) Never mind that the Earth's average temperature hasn't budged for eighteen years, while college costs have risen over 900 percent. Never mind too that, according to experts, even our best efforts to reduce carbon pollution will make less than a degree of difference over the next hundred years. And especially never mind that carbon dioxide is not even a pollutant. Instead it is a chemical needed by plants to make all food and is thus a chemical that sustains *all life* on this planet.

Also never mind that human-induced climate change is far from being *settled* science. In Bill's Laws, I pointed out in a previous blog that bad science has a half-life of about a decade, bad politics a century, and bad religion a millennium. Scares about population bombs and resource scarcity, as well as scares about communism and religion, have followed my laws fairly closely. With the ascent of Green politics and the religious support of Pope Francis, the predicted time frames for the collapse of climate change science may be off a fraction, but my bet is that Bill's Laws number one will still prove valid.

As for education, I have a few suggestions.

1. Stop expanding and start reducing the numbers of students going to college. Paradoxically, do it by offering free government-financed GI Bill–type scholarships at all levels, including elementary and graduate schools—tuition plus stipends for room and board—*but* restrict that support to the genuinely talented. I know this will not be popular, and you may or may not get more diversity. You will get more education. Despite the costs, such a *free* plan would reduce costs in the long run by drastically reducing the college population and improving the educational environment for all schools.

2. Squelch the notion that a college education is the key to higher earnings. It never was a good argument for *higher* learning.
3. Massively expand the opportunities for apprenticeship training and technical schools for average and below-average students who may have the desire but lack the intellectual talent to benefit from a four-year college. These average and below-average young people also deserve increased opportunities for "life, liberty, and the pursuit of happiness."
4. Take seriously the possibilities for increasing efficiency at all education levels by more creative use of computers and the Internet for conveying information instead of relying on outdated classroom and lecture methods. It's scandalous that this has not happened yet.

Populations

● ● ●

Dec. 5, 2011

THE GREEN SUSTAINABLE MOVEMENT IS built on the three claims, all of them false: (1) resources are rapidly dwindling, (2) our industrial system is destroying the planet with pollution, and (3) there are too many people. I will tackle population first.

Like everyone, I worry about overpopulation when I get into a traffic jam; when I have to wait in a long line at the checkout counter; when I drive around Chicago or up the eastern seaboard from Washington to Boston; or when I see riots, famines, oil spills, Occupy Wall Street, or Black Lives Matter demonstrations on my TV. What are these people doing, for heaven's sakes? Why aren't they working or, well, whatever?

On the other hand, when I drive through the plains of Nebraska, Kansas, or North Dakota; the forests of Michigan, Wisconsin, or Maine; the deserts of Arizona, New Mexico, or California; the mountains of Colorado, Utah, or Wyoming, I wonder—where are all the people?

Jane and I have also been fortunate enough to visit the rain forests of Brazil, Southeast Asia, and Ecuador; see the wildlife in South Africa, Kenya, and Tanzania; trek in the mountainous and the desert regions of China, Morocco, Mali, and Turkey; and explore the surprising wild spots of Germany, Italy, the United Kingdom, and France. Beautiful! Where are all the people?

Personal experiences are one thing, serious data another. Here the story is equally clear. The wealthiest, healthiest, best fed, best educated, least crime-ridden, and most creative parts of Earth are also the most densely populated. The poorest, least educated, most diseased, most crime- and most famine-ridden parts of Earth turn out to be the most sparsely populated.

How many people can the resources of planet Earth support with a decent lifestyle? According to some ecological gurus, like Howard Odum, John Holdren, and Paul Ehrlich—one billion at best. An anonymous writer in the *New Yorker* wrote in a 1992 "Talk of the Town" column, "Almost everyone now agrees that if people in the South [the Southern Hemisphere] tried to live as we do in the North, the result would be ecological disaster."

"Almost everyone" does not include me nor an increasing majority of scientific and economic experts around the world. We already have seven billion neighbors, and more than half of that seven now have a decent lifestyle. A minority are still poor but moving rapidly in the rich direction.

Is there a theoretical limit? Of course. The Earth is finite and can't support an infinite number of anything. But that useless exercise in logic highlights the basic fault in the doomsday whine. It is based on Malthus's claim that people multiply geometrically, and resources can increase only arithmetically. The facts show that we have not multiplied geometrically (today native populations in developed countries are decreasing, not multiplying), and resources have not grown arithmetically (today resources are multiplying geometrically virtually everywhere). This error came because Malthus, and his followers today, leave out the most important part of populations and of resources—the creativity of the human hand and mind.

Populations in the wealthy countries of Europe, Japan, and North America have plateaued and, in many cases, are decreasing today. In poorer countries in the tropics, the Southern Hemisphere, and parts of Asia, Africa, and the Middle East, populations are still increasing but at a sharply diminished rate. It is as near certain as anything can be in history that as these countries get richer and move into the Modern Age, their populations will plateau out. We are in no danger of having an infinity of people.

We are living at the dawn, not the twilight, of the scientific-industrial-democratic Modern Age of Earth. Populations *have* exploded in the past two hundred years, just as they did when humans moved from a hunting-gathering lifestyle to an agricultural one. They are leveling off now, just as they did in the early centuries of the Agricultural Age.

In our case, not only has the number of people increased dramatically in the past two hundred years, so, too, life, liberty, and the pursuit of happiness have improved even more dramatically for billions of people. This progress, both in numbers and in quality of life, is truly unprecedented in human history.

Unless you are an incurable misanthrope, how can you want to return to the one billion levels? Do you really want to deny the right to life, liberty, and the pursuit of happiness to six out of seven of your family and neighbors? That's what it amounts to, unless you are also an incurable racist and just want to get rid of six out of seven people of color.

The Earth now has more intelligence and creativity than it had in all of its past ages combined. And most people everywhere—even the ones with limited intelligence and creativity—are better off now than they have ever been in human history. People on Earth today all benefit from less violence, less poverty, better environments, more food, more years of life, more pleasure, more leisure, more travel, less pain, more health care, and more potential for anything and everything. Instead of bemoaning the dramatic increase in populations, we should shout hoorah and hallelujah. It is the greatest story of progress ever told.

It is true that more people means more demand for food and other resources. As the late economist and pioneer researcher on population issues, Julian Simon, wrote, "A human mind seldom comes unaccompanied by a human body." But recent history has clearly shown how powerful creative minds have been in expanding the supply of food and other life-sustaining resources. As a result, seven billion people are better off than one billion were two hundred years ago.

Simon claims,

> Resources come out of people's minds more than out of the ground or air. Minds matter economically as much as or more than hands or mouths. Human beings create more than they use, on average. It had to be so, or we would be an extinct species. These [Malthusian] models simply do not comprehend key elements of people—the imaginative and creative.
>
> This is my long-run forecast in brief, the material conditions of life will continue to get better for most people, in most countries, most of the time, indefinitely. Within a century or two, all nations and most of humanity will be at or above today's Western living standards.
>
> I also speculate, however, that many people will continue to *think and say* that the conditions of life are getting *worse*.[4]

---

[4] Simon, Julian, *The Ultimate Resource* (NJ: Princeton Press, 1981).

Resources...and Wealth

● ● ●

Nov. 4, 2011

A NEW READER, STAN MYERS, retired industrial engineer from Philadelphia and college friend from Antioch, responded to last week's blog: "You have set yourself a difficult challenge to explain why the concept of 'spaceship Earth' having limited human carrying capacity is false. I think it would be easier to refute the laws of gravity. I look forward to the blog that will explain your position."

Stan probably represents the majority opinion among educated people today.

Here goes.

For more than a hundred thousand years, the "human carrying capacity" of our spaceship Earth was low. In hunting/gathering societies, humans were like wolves, tigers, bears, and other carnivores and omnivores—they had territories. Because the territories on Earth were limited, Earth could accommodate only a few million people. And the human accommodations were only marginally better than their competing carnivores and omnivores enjoyed.

Once agriculture and animal husbandry came along in the dawn of recorded history, the carrying capacity of Earth increased dramatically. This Agricultural Age lasted ten thousand years. Many diverse civilizations rose and fell. This same Earth, now aided by a new agricultural technology, could support a hundred times as many people. To be sure, most people had not-very-appealing accommodations. And most led short, labor-intensive lives as slaves, serfs, or peasants.

The next really big change came about the time the United States was born in the late eighteenth century. A little over two hundred years ago, we in the Western world entered the scientific-industrial-democratic Modern Age. Available resources increased spectacularly, and soon the same spaceship could "carry" billions of people—as of last week, seven billion. The Earth had not changed, but two centuries later, a majority of people on the spaceship could live longer, healthier lives with less labor-intensive work in relatively luxurious accommodations.

As to the future, it's hard to predict. Judging from the past, the Earth's resources are not as limited as many believe. They seem to be expandable on demand.

I named my first book, *Twilight or Dawn: A Traveler's Guide to Free-Market Liberal Democracy* (2011). I reported on the comparatively short time humans have had to experiment with this new world of increased carrying power and relative abundance. Many pundits think it is the twilight of the Modern Age. I think it is closer to the dawn and I wrote the book to explain our growing pains.

The reputed founders of modern ecology, Eugene and Howard Odum, based the limited-capacity concept and the sustainability ethic that is popular today on their work with coral reef and freshwater pond ecosystems. We interviewed both Eugene and Howard on videotape before they both died in the late 1990s.

The Odums were correct that energy in and matter in had to equal energy out and matter out. The reefs and the ponds are zero-sum systems. To a limited extent, this was also true of past Hunting/Gathering and Agricultural Age societies. When the Odums (and their "limits to growth" followers) extrapolated the biological findings to the whole Earth, they concluded that the Earth could sustainably support only one billion people. They neglected to factor in the crucial wild card—the power of human creativity.

There is a Chinese proverb: "A peasant must stand on a hillside with his mouth open for a long time before a roast duck flies in."

That's the way it is with resources. If you wait for them to fly ready-made into your life, resources are few. If you search, work, and create, resources can be abundant. This is because the most important ingredients are neither energy nor matter. The ultimate resource is always the human hand and mind.

Energy and matter do count, of course.

In hunting-gathering days, energy was fire and human muscle power, fed by the sun-stored energy of plants and animals. Matter was what could be found by looking. Energy in equaled energy out.

In the Agricultural Ages, energy was still fire and the muscle power of humans, but now animal muscle power was added. It was multiplied now by a new technology of farming and animal husbandry. In later agricultural times, energy in the form of sailing ships, windmills, and waterwheels added to the supply and gave a hint of future plenty. Matter was now anything that could be grown by agriculture with animal help. Energy in still equaled energy out.

When science and technology, free-market capitalism, and liberal democracy began to blossom two hundred years ago, the resource supply for energy soon increased exponentially. Fossil fuels, steam, and internal-combustion engines, along with electricity to transport the energy, increased the carrying capacity of our spaceship exponentially. Matter was now literally any*thing* that could be created in factories using basic atoms and molecules as raw materials.

I can hear critics saying, "Yes, but what about when we run out of fossil fuels and natural resources to feed our factories? And what about the environment and climate change? Aren't we in danger of destroying our planet?"

I will leave the environment, climate change, and the potential destruction of the planet for next week.

As for running out of energy and natural resources—I seriously doubt it. Recent discoveries in the United States and around the world, along with new technology, point to supplies of fossil fuels lasting a few hundred years more, probably longer. (Note: this was written three years ago, when gasoline was approaching five dollars a gallon; today it is closer to two dollars a gallon.) In this country, the only things holding back increased production and use of energy are faulty philosophy and political will. If and when the fossil fuels run out (or are slowed by political will), human ingenuity will no doubt find new sources of energy and new ways to operate our machines more efficiently. We already have nuclear power. Fusion power is on the horizon. Perhaps we will even make a breakthrough in new renewable sources soon. Also note that the iPhone of today (4.8 ounces and $199) is superior in performance to the ENIAC computer (30 tons and $6 million) a few decades ago—and it uses far less energy. Energy-out still equal energy-in as matter-in still equals matter-out, but creative science can always discover new sources of both energy and any particular kind of matter, including food.

The carrying capacity of any spaceship depends not only on energy but also on matter.

People are reluctant to believe it, but we have roughly the same forest resources now that we had two hundred years ago. True, there is not as much virgin forest but there is as much, if not more, harvestable lumber. Metal ores are still abundant, although political will to permit mining them is in short supply. Chemists even tell us that seawater has enough metallic and nonmetallic atoms that once we figure out more efficient ways to concentrate and harvest them, the ocean could supply the world with all of our matter resources for many millennia to come. Seawater is also a prime source of a hydrogen isotope that is a likely future fusion-energy source. And in the more distant future, we may even be able to harvest energy and matter from the moon and asteroid belts.

It is the same story with food. Two hundred years ago, the average farmer could feed the family and half a person more. Today the average farmer in America or Europe can feed a family and more than a hundred people more. Tomorrow we may be able even to make food in factories, feed it to turkeys, and have a Thanksgiving dinner that doesn't require any farmland. We simply have to discover the secret that nature found a billion years age or so ago—how to manage photosynthesis. Water, carbon dioxide, and sunlight are plentiful enough.

For those who still demand "natural" food, we could add organically grown fruits and vegetables to the menu. They could be grown on a tiny fraction of the land needed for present wheat, corn, rice, and soybean crops that mostly feed animals today.

In addition, natural resources are not the same thing as wealth. The Netherlands, Taiwan, and Switzerland have few natural resources but are rich. The Congo, Afghanistan, and North Korea have abundant natural resources but are poor.

Oil is a natural resource; energy is wealth. Forests are a natural resource; lumber is wealth. Sand and metal ores are a natural resource; computers are wealth. Soil, water, and sun are natural resources; food is wealth. A newborn baby is a natural resource; an educated adult is wealth.

To sum up, natural resources are needed, but to turn them into wealth takes creativity and work. If we play our cards right, we will never run out of either.

Finally, I haven't forgotten my friend Stan's other remark: "What is the impact on the natural environment as population increases?" My view is that we need to seek some optimum balance.

Next week I will give my suggestions for the balance.

Environment, Pollution, and Sustainability

● ● ●

Nov. 14, 2011

THE SUSTAINABILITY ETHIC CLAIMS THAT our present industrial system is polluting the Earth and making it increasingly deadly to living things, including people. Some Green zealots even claim the increase in carbon dioxide may destroy our civilization.

Like the previous claim about declining resources, these claims are false. Not only false, but hurtfully so.

No one denies the need for reasonable legislation to control pollution. No one denies the moral responsibility of individuals, companies, and government to clean up your mess after you make it. No one opposes what I call *Light Green*—that is, promoting greater efficiency in all economic activities. The *Dark Green* lobby goes further and demands actions that make things worse instead of better.

For instance, Dark Greens have successfully urged the government to subsidize biofuel, presumably to provide more renewable energy supplies and to protect the environment. Thousands of acres of corn are now devoted to making gasoline instead of food. The predictable result is that the price of food *and* gasoline has risen. Corn, like oil, is a fungible commodity. When the largest producers of corn sharply cut back on their supply by diverting corn to biofuel, the price of corn rises. Gas also gets less efficient and more expensive. The rise in corn prices may not be a serious problem for US consumers. For people in the poorer countries of Latin America, Africa, and Asia, it can be a catastrophe. It pushes millions to borderline starvation.

Many other current subsidies to "clean green power" serve mainly to enrich crony capitalists, increase the deficit, balloon the national debt, and raise the cost of energy to consumers. Because energy is needed for any activity, these subsidies also raise the cost of all products and services and make little if any contribution to controlling carbon dioxide. Far better for our economy and for our environment would be: permitting work to continue on the Keystone XL, the oil pipeline from Canada to Texas; encouraging drilling in coastal waters and Alaska; allow exports of oil, gas, and coal; and speed instead of slow the technology of natural gas reservoirs by new fracking technology. These would all be win-win projects that do not require subsidies, increase efficiency, create productive jobs, lower gas prices, make profits, and help wean us from dependence on imports from countries that are trying to destroy us. Developing the natural gas reservoirs would also help reduce our carbon footprint as well by replacing polluting coal in our power plants.

Rachel Carson's influential book, *Silent Spring*, launched the modern environmental movement a few decades ago. The good news is the book alerted us to the dangers of careless over-use of pesticides and herbicides and saved the lives of some eagles and peregrine falcons. The bad news is it launched a mindless "chemophobia" among large segments of the American and world public, including the mainstream media. The result today is that a majority of the public is suspicious of anything with a "chemical" label.

Dichlorodiphenyltrichloroethane (DDT) won a Nobel Prize for a Swiss chemist in 1948 for its efficacy in saving the lives of millions of US soldiers and other world citizens whose lives would have been lost to malaria and typhus before and during World War II. Arguably It could help in the current Zika mosquito epidemic.

The EPA's own science panel voted against a ban, but in deference to the public outrage after Rachel Carson's book, the EPA director banned

DDT in 1972. Since then, the mosquitoes that transmit malaria (and potentially the new Zika-transmitting mosquitoes) have multiplied, and millions of people in the underdeveloped world of Asia and Africa, especially children, have died from the disease.

It is the same story with other chemical pesticides, herbicides, chemical fertilizers, and, more recently, with genetically engineered (GM) crops and animals. These useful chemicals and technologies have played key roles in providing food and safe drinking water for expanding populations worldwide in the twentieth century with little, if any, scientifically demonstrated harm. Modern chemical and genetically engineered drugs have also alleviated pain and saved millions of lives worldwide, including that of my wife, Jane.

Chemists themselves have innocently contributed to this chemo phobia by finding ways to identify ever-smaller amounts of a given chemical. When people read of the next scary chemical, like lead or copper compounds found in drinking water, they don't stop to consider that "the poison is in the dose."

Pure distilled H_2O can be toxic if taken in large enough quantities. When it is reported that some five hundred tongue-twisting-named chemicals are found in tap water or in the bloodstream of a newborn baby, people are horrified. They want the government to spend whatever it takes to get rid of the last nanogram, not paying attention to the fact that a concentration of a nanogram per liter is equivalent to five grains of salt in Lake Tahoe, or a penny lost in the sand surrounding Lake Michigan. The public falls for every marketer's advertisement or farmer's market sign that the product is "natural," "organic," with "no chemicals added," apparently unaware that all food—in fact, all natural objects including our own bodies and brains—is and always has been constructed of hundreds of thousands of tongue-twisting-named chemicals.

This excessive fear of chemicals easily carries over to excessive fear of radiation. When it comes to the radiation emitted by nuclear waste or a nuclear accident, people and the media panic. For instance, Three

Mile Island, the worst nuclear accident in this country, caused about the same amount of radiation to spread to nearby homes and people as one jet flight across the country brings to passengers. Even the explosion at Chernobyl in the Soviet Union has been vastly exaggerated in its harmful effects by the international media.

Chemophobia and radiation phobia (GM "food phobia" is a recent addition) causes real damage. It has all but destroyed the one technology we already have that could be of significant help in dealing with predicted climate change—nuclear power. It raises the costs of producing all food and drugs. It threatens millions, especially in the undeveloped world, with disease, malnutrition, and starvation. In combination with class-action suits widely advertised on television by unscrupulous class-action lawyers, it brings astronomically higher costs to modern health care and life-saving drugs in the United States and all other countries.

What about the extremist claim that growing pollution in industrial countries is so bad it threatens to destroy our civilization or even nature itself?

According to the most respected world expert on pollution, chemist Bruce Ames at the University of California at Berkeley, this is nonsense. Ames is the inventor of the most widely accepted test for carcinogens and mutagens. "All of whatever I have been learning is telling me that pollution [in this country and most of the industrialized Western world] is pretty much irrelevant to public health. A little problem here and there...but the whole country seems to be thinking that pollution is very important."[5]

A little reading in history will show that in past ages there was indeed horrendous pollution, mostly caused by severe sanitation problems. People used to throw their (organic) garbage in the street. (Organic) horses and pigs, along with tons of their daily (organic) excrement, decorated all the unpaved streets of cities everywhere in the world. Aristocrats used the staircases at Versailles for latrines. As a result,

---

5 Bruce Ames, 1997, Hawkhill video.

epidemics of plague, cholera, typhoid fever, and tuberculosis regularly killed millions of people on all of the Earth's continents.

Closer to today, when I was a young man, most people around the world still heated their homes and apartments with coal. I myself walked the streets of Pittsburgh, Cleveland, New York, and Chicago in the 1940s. The streets were so thick with coal soot and thousands of invisible chemicals (we didn't have the technology then to identify them), that on a winter's day it was even difficult to see across the street when the sun was shining. Rivers, streams, and lakes were regularly used as waste dumps. The Cuyahoga River in Cleveland caught fire not once, but five times—in 1868, 1912, 1936, 1952, and 1969.

To the credit of early environmentalists and sanitary engineers, the air, the water, and the soil in the United States and other Western countries are much cleaner and much safer than they were fifty or even twenty years ago. Despite this progress, the common opinion even among educated people is still strongly influenced by chemo-phobia.

Have all of our environmental problems been solved? Of course not. We need the EPA. But the EPA also needs to strike a reasonable balance between cost and benefit. And above all, we need to get over our irrational chemical phobia, GM phobia, and radiation phobia.

That still leaves what many consider the crucial issue today—the increasing amount of carbon dioxide in the atmosphere that many think will bring catastrophic climate change. This is such an important issue that I plan to postpone the consideration of overpopulation and devote my next week's blog to climate change.

Climate Change

● ● ●

Nov. 21, 2011

Is the increasing amount of carbon dioxide in the atmosphere going to destroy polar bears? Is climate change going to be an unmitigated catastrophe for our civilization and our planet? Are people who disagree "flat-earthers," anti-science cranks, and evolution deniers?

No. No. And no.

I realize most people today [note that this blog was written six years ago] believe the "scientific community" is near unanimous in disagreeing with my three no's.

Most people are wrong.

As Richard Lindzen, a world-class climatologist from the Massachusetts Institute of Technology (MIT) and a member of the United Nations panel on climate change (IPCC), pointed out, "The American Society of Agronomy, the American Society of Plant Biologists and the Natural Science Collection … have no expertise whatever in climate."

These scientific groups are typical of the "overwhelming" scientific opinion that some news media refer to on climate change. Scientists, like the rest of us, are not immune to jumping on bandwagons. Freeman Dyson, a Prize-winning physicist from Princeton, says this about the computer models that are used to analyze data and predict climate change:

> The models solve the equations of fluid dynamics, and they do a very good job of describing the fluid motions of the atmosphere

and the oceans. They do a very poor job of describing the clouds, the dust, the chemistry and the biology of fields and farms and forests. They do not begin to describe the real world we live in.

Dyson speculated on the appeal of the *overwhelming* agreement.

> The books that I have seen about the science and economics of global warming, including the two books under review, miss the main point. The main point is religious rather than scientific. There is a worldwide secular religion, which we may call environmentalism, holding that we are stewards of the Earth, that despoiling the planet with waste products of our luxurious living is a sin, and that the path of righteousness is to live as frugally as possible.[6]

(Pope Francis a few years later jumped on this bandwagon and advised us to "lower our standard of consumption" in order to help the poor and save the Earth.)

Dr. Dyson is not alone in denouncing climate change as a religious, not a scientific, concept. A Nobel Prize physicist, Ivan Glaever, resigned from the American Physical Society (APS), because an official bulletin put out by APS claimed there was "incontrovertible" evidence that human activity is causing the temperature to rise to dangerous levels. Dr. Glaever e-mailed to the APS, "'*incontrovertible*' sounds more like a Papal Bull than a scientific society."

He expanded on this charge, "In the APS it is ok to discuss whether the mass of the proton changes over time and how a multiuniverse behaves, but the evidence of global warming is incontrovertible? The claim (how can you measure the average temperature of the whole Earth for a whole year?) is that the temperature has changed from ~288.0 to ~288.8 degree Kelvin in about 150 years, which (if true) means to me is

---

6 Dyson, Freeman, *Heretical Thoughts about Science and Society* (2006).

that the temperature has been amazingly stable, and both human health and happiness have definitely improved in this 'warming' period."[7]

Many other prominent scientists, including world-respected climatologists like Richard Lindzen, William Gray, Fred Singer, and Roy Spencer, believe the climate-change scare is more religious than scientific. In 2007, here is how Dr. Lindzen, the MIT expert, put it in a Larry King interview:

> We're talking of a few tenths of a degree change in temperature. None of it in the last eight years, by the way. And if we had warming, it should be accomplished by less storminess. But because the temperature itself is so unspectacular, we have developed all sorts of fear of prospect scenarios—of flooding, of plague, of increased storminess when the physics says we should see less. I think it's mainly just like little kids locking themselves in dark closets to see how much they can scare each other and themselves.[8]

All that said, an impressive majority of professional climatologists today (not of meteorologists interestingly enough) do think the evidence for global warming is compelling. Not as many claim it to be *incontrovertible*. A few, like NASA's James Hansen, are so committed to the extremist claims that when asked what would happen if President Obama approved the Keystone XL pipeline from Canada, he replied, "Essentially, it's game over for the planet."

Contrarians like Lindzen and me are not as dogmatic. They agree there has been some warming over the past century. They agree that the CO_2 percentage in the air has risen. Slightly. They don't say global warming is a hoax. Some even agree we should have a carbon tax to provide incentives for renewable alternatives. And no one denies the

---

7 Glaever, Ivan. (see many Internet citations 2007)
8 Lindzen, Richard. Interviews with author (2007)

greenhouse effect is real—without it the Earth would be too cold for life, period.

The debate is not so much about the data (though many do question the recent data as well), but more about what we can expect in the future. Bad-mouthing contrarians as anti-science cranks, evolution deniers, or flat-Earth know-nothings is not helpful.

When scientists make predictions about the future, they are often no better than Ouija-board seers. The astronomer Carl Sagan predicted a nuclear winter would result from the 1991 burning of seven hundred oil wells in Kuwait; the biologist Paul Ehrlich predicted in 1968, "sixty-five million Americans would die of starvation by 1990"; in 1979, a major climate-change proponent, the late Stephen Schneider, "projected that man's potential to pollute will increase 6 to 8-fold in the next 50 years... sufficient to trigger an ice age." (Schneider later changed that to a "Fried Age" instead of an "Ice Age"); scientists making up the Club of Rome and the *Global 2000 Report to the President* (which included physicist John Holdren, the current science adviser to President Obama) predicted we would run out of gasoline and just about everything else before the twentieth century ended.

What can we say for certain about future climate change? Is it going to get warmer? Is it going to get colder? Will there be more violent storms? Will there be fewer violent storms?

Take your pick. If it gets warmer, Canada, Siberia, and the Arctic and Antarctic regions will be winners. If it gets colder...who knows? (Counting, there have actually been fewer hurricanes recently, not more.) No matter what happens, there will be problems. If the past two hundred years are any guide, humans will solve the problems, and somehow we will muddle through. People will create solutions, and we will end up better off than they would have been if there had been no changes.

One thing we can be sure that it is the height of folly to bet substantial portions of the present world's wealth and prosperity (which has brought unprecedented progress to the environment and the people) on *any* projection, whether it is based on science, religion, or throwing the dice.

Eight of the world's most prominent economists, including four Nobel winners, met in Denmark a few years ago at the Copenhagen Consensus. They were challenged to put together an imaginary budget of fifty billion dollars in ways that would be of most benefit to the world's people. They were presented with a list of fifteen global problems and asked to rank them in order and to specify how much of the fifty billion each should receive. To the chagrin of climate change activists, climate change (aka global warming) came out last, taking the fifteenth spot. It would get the least money. In their considered opinion, more than half of the money should go to AIDS research and prevention. The number two priority would be to provide micronutrients such as iron, iodine, and vitamin A to the billions of people who suffer from stunted growth, lower IQ, or blindness because they are not getting adequate nutrition. Number three would be free trade (which would bring the most benefits for the least money). After that came malaria protection, clean water supplies, new agricultural techniques, and the like. All of these would be, in their opinion, of greater potential benefit to more people in the world than wealth sacrificed now to prevent possible global climate change in the future.

Most voters in polls also agree. What do you think?

Intermission

● ● ●

WALKING WITH FRANKIE DOWN EAST Gilman Street to check on the Edgewater Hotel progress, I realized I had Frankie's leash in tightly clenched fists behind my back. I remember seeing an old man in a Mao jacket walking down a street in Kunming, China, with his fists clenched tightly behind his back. Is that the way of old men, communist or capitalist?

I remember too walking across the campus of Notre Dame University when I was a seventeen-year-old recruit in the US Navy V-12 program. That same day the army was landing on the French coast on D-Day, and I felt guilty being safe in college. A professor stopped a buddy and me. He admonished us to walk with a more military step and rhythm. Funny what you remember.

One of my most vivid memories from high school is of a psychology teacher, a Dominican priest, who pointed his finger at a student in the front row and admonished him, "I don't mind if you look at your watch, but please don't shake it to see if it is still running." In that spirit, I dearly hope this book will not tempt you to shake your watch to see if it is still working!

Jane and I go swimming most afternoons at the indoor pools of the Capitol Lakes Aquatic Center. The pools are in an expensive retirement home here in our capital city of Madison, Wisconsin. The pools were a gift from a local philanthropist, who put a condition on the gift—they had to be open to local seniors at a modest fee. In the lap pool, I do six to ten laps with an easy backstroke. It's the time of day I feel most healthy. While on my back in the tepid, ultraclean blue water, gazing up through skylights, I watch the cranes working across the street to build more apartments amid the moving clouds. I close my eyes when the sun breaks through, and I brainstorm ideas. There follow a few examples.

The "Clergy"

● ● ●

Nov. 3, 2014

A FELLOW IDEA MAN AND in-law, Ravi Dykema, in Boulder, Colorado, took offense at a recent blog and e-mailed me,

> Your characterization of college profs as 'clergy' sets them apart as a tribe…and renders them fodder for demonization…I don't think such generalizations are accurate. Just as I don't think the generalizations you attribute to this clergy are accurate: '(The US is) raping and pillaging other countries.' Maybe some professors think or say this, but it is wrong to say that all do. Only if I wanted you to dislike or distrust them would I characterize them all thus. And then my characterization would say more about me than about them…Educated or not educated?—'Cops are pigs. Politicians are crooks. Northerners are elitist. School just makes you into a pawn of the system.'

I agree with Ravi that not all cops are pigs, not all politicians are crooks, and not all northerners are elitists. Not sure I understand "school just makes you a pawn of the system." I agree, too, that not all professors are liberal clergy. If I implied otherwise, I apologize to the few conservative or libertarian ones. As for the insult implied by the name *clergy*, I doubt many religions today would feel that calling their leaders *clergy* would be "fodder for demonization."

I do say that *most* professors today—not all—are members and often leaders of a new secular religion. They are "clergy" in the sense that they set the tone, the agenda, and the ideal for political, social, and religious debate in this country, just as the Catholic clergy did in medieval days. This modern clergy don't wear any special garb, and there are no popes or bishops, but they do teach faith in a new secular religion—call it Green-Progressive.

Green-Progressives don't have an imprimatur or Index of Forbidden Books, although peer reviewing and political correctness are close cousins. They don't have a reigning College of Cardinals but the Ivy League is a good approximation. With only a few exceptions, Green-Progressives dominate the modern education, publishing, media, and entertainment world—even the scientific establishment. An astonishingly high percentage of executive decision makers (Supreme Court justices for instance) come from the Ivy League or a few other elite colleges (faint echoes of the College of Cardinals?), and a good percentage, I hesitate to say it, are Jews. I don't demonize them. I was once a member of this august clergy, and I still believe in much of the basic dogma.

With Green-Progressives, I too believe that democracy is the best political system yet devised; science and technology are important and good; we should be tolerant of religious, racial, sexual, and lifestyle differences; all people are created equal under the law and we should do our very best to provide equal opportunities for all. I agree further that exclusive monotheistic and supernatural religious dogmas have no place in the Modern Age, but we should nevertheless respect individuals of all cultures and faiths; we should reduce pollution and protect our environment; and, finally, we should err on the optimistic and generous side rather than the doomsday and miserly one (this last faith is often opposed by some of the more radical Green members of the modern clergy).

This Green-Progressive clergy centered in the elite universities, non-profit world, and government bureaucracy can take some credit for the economic growth in the second half of the twentieth century—and special credit for the truly amazing progress of talented women and minorities (the freedom riders and civil rights activists helped here). Not to mention the progress we have made in reducing pollution has made our environment better and safer than ever before (with help from the Sierra Club, wealthy patrons, and so on).

There have been other significant contributors to our social progress. Number one unquestionably is greater wealth, thanks to a growing economy. Number two may well be more and better education. Number three may paradoxically, be inequality (which correlates strongly with economic growth!). Number four is the government, larger and more active in combating bigotry than ever before (it led the way in abolishing slavery in a Civil War; later, in some states at least, it *promoted* bigotry with Jim Crow laws; still later it helped to control and lessen bigotry with national civil rights laws). Number five may be major banks and corporations—larger, more profitable, and with more influence than ever before. I leave it to the statisticians and sociologists to tease out the respective contributions each of these factors has made to our progress.

Many Green-Progressive educators today go further and teach extreme, false, and reactionary views with scant evidence. For example: that education is a panacea; profit-making business is questionable, non-profit is better; that the United States is exceptional only in its penchant for violence and its historical and present-day embrace of feminist, racial, and sexual bigotry; that other cultures may be equal or superior to our Western one; that equal opportunity for minorities is not enough—we need equal results; that white privilege is rampant, and only when people of color gain power will it fade; that demand, not supply, drives the economy; that individuals don't build a business; governments do; that organic and natural is way to go; that GM, nuclear, chemical, and IQ sciences are flawed and dangerous; that ecology and environmental sciences are profound and trustworthy; that the middle class is suffering as inequality soars; that higher minimum wages will reduce inequality and help the middle class; that overpopulation, resource scarcity, and pollution (climate change) are the world's most serious problems; and believing all this, it follows that sustainability, not growth, is the ideal. This last dogma is the one most fervently held by Greens. It also has the weakest evidence from the newest and most uncertain of the sciences—climatology, ecology, and environmental studies.

Radical leaders like Bill McKibben, Paul Ehrlich, Noam Chomsky, and their followers carry the above dogmas to greater extremes. Chomsky, for instance, claims the United States has been and still is the world's greatest terrorist state, continually and unmercifully guilty of raping and pillaging other countries. He says of 9/11, "We had it coming." Ehrlich says if we don't reduce the world population soon, from seven billion to one billion, we are doomed. (So far as I know, he has no real plan how to do this.) McKibben too thinks we are witnessing a catastrophic "end of nature" with our carbon pollution. (He does have a plan—abolish fossil fuels—and some zealots think that approving even one more oil pipeline means death for the natural world.)

Ravi is right. The extreme views in that last paragraph are not held or taught by all professors or even by a majority. They are not totally dismissed or rejected either. A poll during Reagan's term showed the University of Wisconsin-Whitewater faculty were unanimous (not even one dissenter) in opposing Reagan's Cold War policies—policies that snubbed noses at most Green-Progressive dogmas and policies that more important, succeeded.

I almost forgot. Most Green-Progressives believe government is best when the Democratic Party is in control. In college towns like Madison and Boulder, Green-Progressives combine with unions, trial lawyers, and crony capitalists to make sure the Democratic Party has that power permanently.

The Clergy—Who, What, and Why?

• • •

Feb. 15, 2016

I OFTEN WRITE DISPARAGINGLY OF the modern clergy. Exactly what is this clergy? Why do I call them clergy? And who are they, anyway?

Perhaps I should distinguish between the Progressive and the Green clergy but they overlap a lot. The same individual can typically be found in both camps (and he or she seldom recognizes the contradictions).

Progressive clergy believe on faith: (1) Western civilization is only one of many civilizations and is not superior (multiculturalism); (2) capitalism is suspect; socialism is better; and social-welfare democracy, as in Europe, may well be the best compromise; (3) people are created equal, so we need equal outcomes as well as equal opportunities.

I am not a Progressive because I don't believe for a minute in (1) and (3), and I have serious problems with (2).

The Green clergy believe on faith that (1) the country and the world are severely overpopulated; (2) we are fast running out of natural resources; and (3) pollution, especially carbon pollution, is threatening to destroy our world. It follows that "a growing economy means a shrinking ecosystem."

I am not a Green because I don't believe in any of these dogmas.

Who does believe them?

Most professors and administrators in elite and not-so-elite colleges, universities, and nonprofit foundations; most media stars and wannabes in California, New York, Washington, and college cities; most government bureaucrats; many teachers in public and private schools; most trial lawyers and union leaders; many Wall Street financiers and large corporate CEOs; most social workers, artists, musicians, writers, entertainers, and actors; most Democrats, many Republicans; and almost all street activists.

Leaders who do believe include Barack and Michelle Obama, Bernie Sanders, Hillary and Bill Clinton, George Bush, Mitt Romney, John McCain, Al Gore, Jimmy Carter, Pope Francis, Elizabeth Warren, Joe Biden, Eric Holder, Paul Ehrlich, John Holdren, Bill McKibben, Paul Krugman, George Soros, Warren Buffett, Jeff Immelt, Michael Bloomberg, Steven Spielberg, Al Sharpton, Steven Colbert, Dan Rather, Noam Chomsky, Whoopi Goldberg, Beyoncé Knowles-Carter, Paul Newman, Oprah Winfrey, Robert Redford. The list of believers includes the late FDR, LBJ, JFK, Richard Nixon, Walter Cronkite, Edward R. Murrow, Arthur Miller, Allen Ginsberg, Norman Mailer, Ernest Hemingway, Berthold Brecht, Howard Zinn, Rachel Carson, Pablo Picasso, Jackson Pollock, Leonard Bernstein, Muhammad Ali, John Lennon, and many, many more. As you can see, a considerable group.

This Progressive-Green Clergy includes the majority of the media and nonprofit world: the *New York Times,* the *New Yorker,* the *Wall Street Journal* (leaving out the editorial pages), the *New Republic,* the *Atlantic,* the *Huffington Post* (with its all female editorial staff), CBS, NBC, ABC, PBS, CNN, the Sierra Club, MoveOn.org, NAACP, ACLU, Black Lives Matter, Occupy Wall Street, Planned Parenthood, the Ford Foundation, the Union of Concerned Scientists, People for the American Way, large segments of the Catholic Church, secular and Reformed Jews, pro-Jewish organizations, and many, many others.

I'm not implying *all* of the clergy agree 100 percent of the time, but on the dogmas it's pretty close. They may differ significantly on details or implementation, as the Christian and Muslim clergy did in medieval times and still do today.

Though not a majority of the population at large, they dominate the education, media, government, entertainment, and science of the country. Whether discussing climate change, economics, lifestyles, information, government policy, education, entertainment, sports, sustainability or technology, the Progressive-Green clergy call the shots, massage the tone, and set the agenda.

They are opposed by a contrarian and motley crew: the *Wall Street Journal* editorial pages, Fox News, the Drudge Report, a few conservative magazines and foundations, the Koch brothers, talk radio, Hillsdale College, and a few conservative or libertarian intellectuals like me. We have the high road often but are low in numbers. Surprisingly enough, we often win local, state, and federal elections. For instance, in the recent primaries for the presidential election, Conservative and Libertarian candidate polled far more votes than Progressive and Green candidates did. Progressives and Greens typically blame the Koch brothers' money for their losses (they seldom mention the big money they collect from unions, Wall Street, and rich individual investors like George Soros and Warren Buffett). They enjoy reveling in their hatred of Fox News (which leads in cable viewers by a goodly margin).

The clergy has other problems today. The *New York Times* and most other Progressive publications have to rely heavily on advertising from conservative corporations and rich individuals to support their Progressive staffs. Bernie Sanders may be a maverick in getting money from the people. Alas, the people are fickle. Popular today is passé tomorrow.

Besides electoral defeats, the dominant left-liberal clergy have other, more serious problems today. Their signature issues, inequality and climate change, are in serious conflict. To help one, you harm the other.

Progressive-Green Pope Francis, for instance, preaches that all citizens in the rich West should "reduce their present level of consumption" in order to help the poor and save the Earth. Yet the pope flies by jet with large carbon footprints to the far corners of Earth to spread his gospel. And while humble personally, he chooses to live in a rich Vatican City environment. President Obama, too, flies often in luxurious private jets, with large carbon footprints, to politic or just to golf in Hawaii and other far-off spots, and sends his wife along with daughters, friends, and celebrities on lavish shopping trips to Spain, London, and Africa.

Obama and Pope Francis are not unusual. Middle and Upper Class Progressives and Greens routinely ignore advice to "reduce their level of consumption." Hillary Clinton, for example, was chided by Bernie Sanders for accepting $650,000 for a single speech to Goldman Sachs; she and her husband, Bill, were paid many times that for speeches to wealthy groups. Their lame excuses were, "That's what they offered" (Hillary) and "We have to pay our bills" (Bill). Green hero Al Gore has multiple mansions and makes big money from crony-capitalist investments in Green technology. The average middle-class Green probably has a second home—at minimum a condo in Florida or Arizona or a cabin in the woods or the Colorado ski country. Even Bernie Sanders, the poor man who has never held a private-sector job and has a modest income, managed to spend months on an Israeli kibbutz in his youth and went to the Soviet Union for his second honeymoon. All that world travel does not make him totalitarian communist/socialist, but it does add substantially to his carbon footprint.

My guess is that like the communists, the Progressives and Greens will end up a sad and forgotten footnote on the march to the Modern Age.

"Slump? I Ain't in No Slump...I Just Ain't Hitting."

• • •

Nov. 2, 2015

I FEEL LIKE THE LATE Yogi Berra. "Slump? I ain't in no slump...I just ain't hitting."

Yogi was a great baseball player and manager with a gift for quotable lines. "I usually take a two-hour nap from one to four." Or "Nobody goes there, anymore. It's too crowded." "If people don't come to the ballpark, how are you going to stop them?" "It's like deja-vu, all over again." And finally, "I really didn't say everything I said."

I have had a long running e-mail battle with an engineering professor from Texas, Michael Sadler. Apparently he is a member of the academic branch of the modern clergy. I deduce that because he vehemently objects to my frequent attacks on sustainability. I could argue, like Yogi, that I really didn't say everything I said. But I'll stick to my guns.

For example, Dr. Sadler not only questioned evidence I sent him from the libertarian Cato Institute. They take money from the Koch brothers, so he claimed that disqualified them from serious consideration. Worse, it caused him to doubt my integrity!

Maybe I'm not hitting very well these days, but Dr. Sadler, like John Holdren (Obama's science adviser) and many other Green Sustainable fans, have an even lower batting average. Physicist Holdren, for instance, led the clergy on doomsday issues like overpopulation, running out of resources, technology scares, DDT, nuclear power (fortunately, Dr. Sadler doesn't agree there), and so on. Doom didn't result from any of these scares. Green fans strike out often.

Most Democrats nowadays agree with Michael Sadler that taking money from the Koch brothers is bad. They (excluding Bernie Sanders) don't object to taking money from billionaire George Soros, unions, Wall Street hedge funds, or rich trial lawyers. Nor do they object to the Clintons taking money for charitable foundations from radical Muslim countries like Saudi Arabia, Kuwait, and Yemen. At least the Koch brothers do not keep women as servants or slaves, nor do they want to deliberately kill us. Democrats also get a whole lot of money from politically naïve Hollywood celebrities who don't have the time, inclination, or intelligence to do much serious reading. This includes actors, directors, and producers like Whoopi Goldberg, Robert Redford, Quentin Tarantino, Oliver Stone, Michael Moore, Oprah Winfrey, Susan Sarandon, and Barbra Streisand.

The Koch brothers' money is different because it comes from oil and gas profits.

Another liberal friend from college, like Dr. Sadler, dismissed evidence from Massachusetts Institute of Technology climatology expert Richard Lindzen for a similar reason. (Lindzen is a prominent world-class scientist who was a member of the International Panel on Climate Change, the UN committee.) He is also, like me, a global warming contrarian. The clergy dismiss Lindzen because he was once was paid for lectures to oil companies. They don't dismiss their friends who routinely get paid for lectures to environmental groups, crony capitalists, or Wall Street speculators who profit handsomely from solar energy boondoggles.

Again, oil companies are different because their money comes from fossil fuel profits.

The assumptions that environmental groups are pure like religions and not influenced by money is naïve indeed. In many ways, environmental groups *are* religions. They believe in dogmas you must accept on faith with skimpy evidence. They are nonprofit and they don't pay taxes. They have their own clergy. But it's a great myth that they, and most other religions, secular and theistic, are pure, unselfish, and not influenced by money. All religions, environmental groups, nonprofit foundations, nonprofit art and business groups, not to mention all schools and colleges, live or die from member dues, government grants, taxes, tuitions, and donors. The donors—government agencies, students, members, and public at large—favor the causes that get the most publicity. In the past these have been Three Mile Island, Love Canal, gasoline shortages, Alar on apples, lead in water and paint, and species extinction. Today it is climate change and sustainability.

The competition is intense to be the "greenest" campus, department, religion, or nonprofit group. The fall issue of *Sierra Club* magazine featured a cover article called "The Ten Coolest Schools." Schools compete to be the most sustainable, who gets the most energy from clean sources; serves the most organic food; has the fewest parking spaces; uses the least plastic, paper and "chemicals"; diverts the most waste from landfills; offers the most courses in sustainable ecology; and so forth and so on.

Environmental organizations and even many commercial corporations compete to see who is most aggressive in jumping on the latest doomster bandwagon. Causes like population, resource scarcity, gasoline shortage, DDT, nuclear power plants, Love Canal, and lead in paint (as I write, lead in drinking water is the newest scare) have lost much of their power to get donor cash. Most donors are also unaware that this is largely due to unpredicted success and subsequent irrelevance rather than the predicted doom that their money was elicited to avoid. Climate change and sustainability are the current winners in the donor sweepstakes—and in television and print advertising.

Despite gloomy predictions of scientists like Holdren and Ehrlich, enterprising scientists and companies using new technologies and fossil fuels made sure that food, energy, and most commodities are cheaper and more plentiful today than ever before in human history. Peregrine falcons and bald eagles were saved with the banning of DDT, but millions of humans in India and Africa died because DDT was not available to help prevent malaria. Zika-carrying mosquitoes are causing birth defects now but can't expect much help from DDT. Alar and Love Canal were harmless, but tell that to the apple growers and homeowners who went bankrupt when doom was in the news. Gasoline is cheap now, and SUVs and luxury cars are more popular. Nuclear power is getting more accepted now and could provide alternative energy in abundance with no CO_2, but many Green-Progressives still oppose it. Lead in children's blood is a current scare, but this, too, may prove more scare than real danger.

Despite their abysmal batting averages, Green partisans think they have a winner now in climate change. Here the alleged villains are the most useful and popular chemicals on Earth—fossil fuels—chemicals that have given people everywhere the energy equivalent of a thousand slaves. Yet the people who provide those chemicals—the Koch brothers, ExxonMobil, Shell, and the like, along with their millions of workers—are demonized. If you take any money from them, you gamble with your integrity.

By rights it should be the other way around. The Koch brothers, ExxonMobil, and other fossil fuel companies along with their many thousands of workers, are the true heroes of our times. They certainly have the highest batting averages. In fact, they are in great measure responsible for the very existence of the Modern Age. The Green clergy, on the other hand, want to lead us back to the Agricultural Age, where religions were top dogs; either the Christian and Muslim clergy were in charge, and beheadings, famines, and plagues were rampant. Green folks do not of course *mean* to lead us there, but as people say—good intentions often pave the road to you know where.

What Would Lincoln Do?

• • •

Feb. 22, 2016

President's Day (and Lincoln's birthday) was last week.

Lincoln's most famous speech ends, "that this nation, under God, shall have a new birth of freedom—and that government of the people, by the people, for the people, shall not perish from the earth."

What would Lincoln think and do today?

Lincoln was our first Republican president. He would never have been nominated today since party bosses, not primary elections, brokered his nomination in Chicago in 1860. The issues, of course, are also very different today, and he might not only fail to be nominated, but like many of us, he would be baffled.

Lincoln was not a big churchgoer, but often, as in the quote above, he did call on God to support him and the country. He knew his Bible, had a strong belief in fate and individual morality. He might well be sympathetic to evangelical Christian voters today insofar as they support individual moral goals and methods. I think he would balk at some of their more extreme positions. As a candidate for Congress on the Whig ticket, for instance, he ran against a Democratic clergyman, Peter Cartwright. The exchange that follows is instructive on his religious bent.

"I observe," preached Cartwright, "that many responded to the first invitation to give their hearts to God and go to heaven. And I further observe that all of you save one indicated that you did not desire to go to hell. The sole exception is Mr. Lincoln, who did not respond to either invitation. May I inquire of you, Mr. Lincoln, where you are going?"

"I came here as a respectful listener," replied Lincoln. "I believe in treating religious matters with due solemnity...Brother Cartwright asks me directly where I am going...I am going to Congress."

He did. And served one undistinguished term.

Would he still be a Republican today?

I can't see him supporting Donald Trump for the nomination. Trump is too arrogant, too prejudiced, and he can't put three words together in a decent sentence. Lincoln was humbler, was not a bigot, and was a master of language. I think Lincoln might support Rand Paul, Marco Rubio, John Kasich, Ben Carson, or even Jeb Bush. He might even have supported Bush's brother and father in the Gulf, Afghanistan and Iraq Wars since he, too, was opposed to oppression. He was also used to being called nasty names, and did not flinch in a war that took not five thousand but over five *hundred* thousand lives.

However, it's not certain. He might *not* have supported Bush in those Middle Eastern wars. As a young congressman, he opposed a war with Mexico that he called "immoral, proslavery, and a threat to the nation's republican values." In those 19th century days it should be noted that a war with Mexico was really none of our business, since literally *every* country in the world was opposed to democracy, and we stood alone as "the last best hope of Earth."

Lincoln was firmly opposed to slavery ("As I would not be a slave, so I would not be a master") but he was not a radical abolitionist. Today his view might well be labeled racist. Lincoln was dead set against prejudice, but he did believe African Americans and white Americans, as groups, not as individuals, could never be equal socially or intellectually. He once even considered a solution that would send emancipated slaves back to West Africa. He could never have been elected today with those views.

Lincoln was our most compassionate president but also one of the most realistic. If he were alive today, I think he would wholeheartedly support Martin Luther King Jr.'s dream that "my children would be judged by the content of their character and not the color of their skin." However, he would not support Al Sharpton or Jesse Jackson in their blanket condemnations of police in Ferguson, New York, Chicago, or Baltimore. And most certainly, he would not support the Progressive dogma that we need to strive for equal outcomes. He might support equal opportunities, but even here he would be skeptical of how we are going to make that a reality.

What would Lincoln think and do about economics and inequality?

Lincoln was a self-taught lawyer and often represented corporations, so it is safe to guess he would lean toward the capitalist Republican side today. However, as President he gave a lot of land away in the Homestead Act of 1862; he did a lot for industry and infrastructure; and he gave a lot of support to land-grant universities in their, "teaching of practical agriculture, military science, and engineering ('without excluding... classical studies')." So Lincoln did think, like modern Democrats, that the government could *help* citizens.

What about the environment?

In his youthful days in New Salem, Illinois, Lincoln was big on infrastructure. To young Lincoln, that meant clearing the Sangamon River for commercial traffic. Later, as a young lawyer, he helped expand railroads across the country.

I wrote a play *A. Lincoln* years ago. In it I imagined,

> When Abraham Lincoln lived in Illinois
> he rode the circuit out over the plains
> where the big blue-stemmed grass bent in the sun.
> Prairie sage and yarrow clogged the fencerow
> and in the autumn spikes of goldenrod, aster
> and devil's hawkweed blazed the uncut meadows.

I admit now that was a bit poetic and fanciful. As president, he had enough to do dealing with the war over slavery, shepherding the Homestead

Act, the education land grants, industry, and railroad expansion that he could not worry that much about environmental issues. Also, we did not have in his day the technology to detect minute quantities of chemicals or radiation in the environment. Based on his pioneer background, Lincoln likely would be sympathetic to conservation issues, but based on his support of the Constitution, his rationality, and his hatred of hypocrisy, I doubt whether he would be a devout Green today.

In summation, I wager that Lincoln, if he were alive today, would be a libertarian Republican like me.

Pearl Harbor

● ● ●

Dec. 7, 2015

Jane and I are members of the fast-disappearing World War II veteran generation. We each served two years during the war, Jane in the US Marines, I in the US Navy. Today we both get our health care from the local VA hospital. Which incidentally is outstanding.

I was a freshman in high school on Sunday, December 7, 1941. It was a warm day in southern Ohio and I was playing touch football in the street when Pat, my younger sister, came out of our house on Rustic Road in Dayton to tell me she just heard on the radio that Japan had bombed Pearl Harbor in Hawaii. I wasn't sure where Hawaii was, much less Pearl Harbor, but I was shocked that the small country of Japan (which most of us thought of then as makers of the most worthless sort of junk) would dare to attack the mighty United States.

People get upset nowadays when terrorists murder innocent people. It's understandable. More people lost their lives when al-Qaeda brought down the World Trade center (three thousand) than were killed when the Japanese bombed Pearl Harbor (two and a half thousand). Recent attacks by radical Muslims in Paris and in San Bernardino took 150 lives, although the terrorist who attacked Planned Parenthood in Colorado killed only three people.

In those world war days, it was *good* news if only three—or, for that matter, only three hundred or even three thousand—were killed. In a single battle for the tiny island in the Pacific called Iwo Jima, our marines had more than twenty-six thousand casualties. On the D-Day landing in France, 425,000 men were killed or wounded. I'll never forget my sobs when, in my sixties, Jane and I visited the American cemetery by Omaha Beach in France, where so many young men my age found their final home furnished only with a small cross. We also tend to forget the millions of innocent civilians in Allied and German bombing raids, as well as the millions of soldiers on both sides in World War II. And Japan too lost millions of soldiers and sailors and millions of innocent civilians in cities from the firebombs in Tokyo and nuclear ones in Hiroshima and Nagasaki.

And then, of course, there was the bloodiest war of all, which my great-grandfather fought in to abolish slavery. Over five hundred thousand men died in that war.

You could always say with Uncle Joe Stalin, the man who was also responsible for millions of civilian deaths in his own country, "A single death is a tragedy; a million deaths is a statistic."

Even many pacifists agree that World War II was a necessary evil. What would the world be like if the Nazis and the Japanese had won?

A streaming video series from Amazon based on a science-fiction novel by Philip K. Dick, *The Man in the High Castle*, tries to answer that question. My son Andrew suggested it. I don't usually care for science fiction (like playing tennis without a net), but Andrew is right, this one is a thriller. The series suggests that if the Nazis and the Japanese had won World War II, the United States would be divided into three parts: an eastern section occupied by Nazi Germany, a western part occupied by Imperial Japan, and a vaguely defined mountainous section in the middle as a buffer zone.

Most people assume that our victory was inevitable. Not so. If Hitler had developed a nuclear bomb before we did (in this fictional version the Nazis wiped out Washington, DC, with a hydrogen bomb); if Germany had invaded and conquered Great Britain when they had the chance in 1941 (Germany had already conquered most of Europe by then, and England had lost most of its army); or if the Japanese had followed up their Pearl Harbor victory and invaded California, our world today would be very different.

One small change: I would not be writing these blogs attacking a reigning clergy that at its best is tolerant and compassionate today. Under the Nazis and Japanese, both the Green-Progressive clergy and I would be in jail or worse. The fictional series makes clear that the occupying government is all-powerful. The series does not address environment, education, climate change, health care (it does touch on this peripherally), welfare, investment, national debt, or basic economic issues. But it makes clear that all of these would be very different with the Japanese and Nazis in charge.

Healthcare for, instance, would be much cheaper. We would not care for invalids, gays, the homeless, handicapped, or the elderly. They don't contribute to production, so they would be simply gassed and cremated. One scene shows young people in the movie living with the annoying smoke from the nearby crematories.

The government would control all education. There would be no private schools or colleges. All education would be state controlled, free, cruel, and racist. There would be few welfare issues. The homeless and the dependent would be sent to slave labor camps or gassed and cremated.

Nazi and Japanese overlords would not permit any immigration or terrorism. Citizens could travel inside the country but not easily (everyone would need identification papers to travel anywhere). Foreign travel would be forbidden or severely restricted. There would not be any places to go that were freer. As for immigrants and refugees, legal or illegal—they would simply not exist.

The fictional series is silent on the environment, and I'm not certain how the topic would be treated in this fictional history. The Nazis as well as the Imperial Japanese actually favored the organic (Hitler was a vegetarian) and promoted the natural virtues of exercise, robust health, good diet, dangerous alpine sports, and hiking in the wilderness. Both the Germans and the Japanese are known even now for obsessive order, cleanliness, and large Green political parties. It's a good guess that the occupying powers would not be that much different from the present-day Green clergy on pollution, wilderness protection, species preservation, and climate change. Whatever the policies and laws, they would be compulsory with severe penalties for noncompliance, including death.

The series writers do not say much about the economy. The occupied country looks prosperous enough but also looks deeply pessimistic. Unemployment, infrastructure, national debt, and growth of the economy do not seem to be major concerns though. There are private companies, factories, and capitalist enterprises, but government offices and bureaucrats are plainly in charge and are far more powerful than private bankers, executives, or financiers. Everyone seems to assume wealth is a fixed thing, and it is the government that decides who gets what and how much. The national mood is doom and gloom. The United States is no longer a world leader, not even "from behind." The economy seems to be a variety of totalitarian fascism or communism/socialism.

I hate to say it (I got my usual surprise in the very writing of this blog!), but except for the extreme and cruel racism—a big exception, I know, but a moral one not a structural one—the United States under Nazi and Japanese occupation would be similar to the one that the left-liberal democratic clergy wants today. The government is firmly in charge of education, health care, housing, food, immigration, the economy, culture, entertainment, media, investment, industry, banking, the environment, elections, police, guns, even the weather and climate—in a word—everything. In another word—fascism.

The truth is Democratic idol FDR in the Great Depression of the 1930s was known to admire—before the war—Italy's fascism, as did many left-liberals.. FDR's National Recovery Act (NRA) was patterned after Italian fascism with tight government control of prices, wages, and industry. (Fortunately, a conservative Supreme Court declared the NRA unconstitutional in 1935, but many of its ideas survived in the New Deal and later Progressive legislation, including current efforts.)

Force is force, coercion is coercion, and whether we use it for a noble cause or an ignoble one, force does work. For a while. Even when it doesn't hurt or kill, it stifles freedom and diversity and brings the Modern Age to a screeching halt.

Whom Do You Trust?

• • •

Jan. 28, 2013

W<small>HEN WE WOKE UP ONE</small> day last week, my wife, Jane, gave me a jolt when she claimed she didn't trust anybody except Frankie (our dog) and Beatrice (our cat). Later she added me, but qualified it with "mostly." At my age, I don't believe she is suspicious of an affair, but who knows.

We both agreed that we could trust our dog and our cat and, for that matter, most animals, who do what they do and only rarely try to deceive you.

With humans you need to beware—there are all levels and varieties of trust.

Despite her words, I think both Jane and I tend to err more on the naïve, trusting side than the cynical, mistrustful one. In our years together, we have traveled to many foreign countries and almost never had any anti-American experiences. When you treat people with respect and trust, they reciprocate. Pretty simple, really. Usually.

When you get beyond the personal, it gets more complex.

Few people put much trust in advertisements or sales pitches. Sometimes we do pay attention, though, and we want to believe that salespeople know what they are talking about. There is an automatic safety valve here—you know they have self-interest, and you make allowances.

However, when someone comes to your door to help you, you're not as sure: Jehovah's Witness or Mormon missionaries; politicians *informing* you on the issues while seeking your vote; environmental activists with a petition; or government agents wanting to *help you* out. I don't know about you, but I often feel like Henry David Thoreau who wrote, "I want to run for my life."

Religion, politics, and science—all of these are tougher when it comes to trust. It is not that politicians, scientists, or clergy deliberately lie to you. Well, sometimes they do. But more often it is the nature of the beast that makes for doubt.

Religious people say that, above all, they trust God's words in the Bible. Usually they are selective, though. They trust the passages that promise love and eternal life but ignore the ones that praise slavery, recommend sinners be stoned to death, or claim God destroyed an entire city or tribe because of wickedness. (Muslims, too, are selective, but, alas, many today do pay attention to the nastier passages in their versions of God's words in the Quran.)

As for politics, our US Constitution is the gold standard. It was not perfect in its original version, but it has been amended to correct most faults. It has been also stretched and interpreted by the Supreme Court. With amendments and interpretations, it has proven to be a fairly trustworthy guide, or at least more so than everyday executive or legislative branch politicians, whether Democrat or Republican.

Science is in many ways the most difficult to assess. Most of us are not scientists and even those who are scientists are usually specialized in a particular branch of science and seldom are proficient outside their specialty. While we tend to trust scientists as a group (as advertising executives know), our trust is not total or universal.

Most of us trust physical scientists and engineers most of the time. It was not always so, but they have a history of remarkable success going back a few centuries. Today when we get into a car, bus, train, or airplane, we trust that the scientists, engineers, and manufacturers knew what they were doing and did a good job in the design and building of our vehicles, roads, bridges, gas stations, airports, even the parking lots. We trust the architects and builders of our houses, apartments, factories, and office buildings. We trust the elevators, escalators, furnaces, stoves, refrigerators, tools—indeed, all the many motors and appliances that all of us depend on today. When failure, or even disaster, does strike, we trust the scientists and engineers to figure out what went wrong and fix it promptly.

When it comes to medicine and biological sciences, our trust weakens a bit. Most of us trust our doctors, nurses, and surgeons, but some doubt creeps in and for good reason. In the millennia before Louis Pasteur, Robert Koch, and other life-science pioneers of the late nineteenth century, you probably would have been better off to steer clear of doctors if you got sick. More often than not, doctors caused more pain, disease, and premature death than they helped avoid or cure. Fortunately and for the most part, that is not true today.

Trust is weakest, and deservedly so in my mind, in the social and environmental sciences.

The social sciences—economics, political science, history, sociology, and the like—try hard to qualify as science by using empirical evidence and a lot of statistics. Despite some progress, the practical conclusions from their research are uncertain, widely debated, and there is little consensus. Pundits often write, "History proves thus and so." Few believe them. Liberal studies corroborate liberal biases. Conservatives studies corroborate conservative biases. Because there are many more liberals in the social sciences than conservatives, I personally remain skeptical of all social-science studies.

I admit to particular skepticism of social-science studies because so often today they have a Marxist base. Karl Marx was a genius and did have some insights, but on the whole his influence has led to some of the most tyrannical and odious regimes of the Modern Age.

Ecology, climatology, and the other environmental sciences are the newest kids on the block. They hardly existed when I was in college. They have not been nearly as time-tested as other sciences have. Despite that lack, many people, scientists and nonscientists alike, often trust their more radical conclusions as if they came from a secular bible.

For instance, President Obama (as well as many others in the media and the general population) claims that "the overwhelming verdict of science" supports his belief in catastrophic climate change. In doing so he is lumping together six million or so physical and biological scientists with a few hundred experts in climatology. In other words, less than a 0.001 percent of scientists are experts in climate science. Obama and the mainstream media don't tell you that there are substantial doubts even among that tiny percentage about the *future* of world climate.

All climatologists agree that global warming and the greenhouse effect are real; that carbon dioxide in the atmosphere has increased; that the Earth has warmed over the last century (about one degree centigrade). But there is lively debate about what that means or does not mean for the Earth's future in the short run and in the long run. The closest field to climatology, meteorology (older and many times larger) is even more conflicted. Over half of meteorologists do not support that overwhelming verdict on catastrophic climate change.

Scientists are human beings and subject to some of the same kind of herd instincts as the rest of us. As a group, they are probably more sensitive to evidence issues, but they also tend to support one another's disciplines. If the climatologists say it is so, the plant biologists, particle physicists, and the electrical engineers tend to agree it must be so. Although it may be true that the overwhelming majority of physicists, chemists, biologists, and engineers support the findings of the climatologists, most members of that majority have no more expertise in climate science than does Barack Obama, CBS News, Bill Stonebarger, or you, dear reader.

When it comes to many controversial environmental issues of past decades, the overwhelming verdict of environmental science turned out to be ludicrously wrong: the population *bomb* of the 1960s was going to lead to massive famines around the world, and millions in the United States were going to starve to death before the twentieth century ended; pesticides were going to poison the Earth, and we would have *silent springs*; oil and gas were going to run out, making our factories and vehicles useless; acid rain was going to destroy our lakes and forests; minerals, land, and all natural resources were going to be in such short supply worldwide that catastrophe was certain; nuclear wastes and accidents were going to poison the whole earth's environment. Today the same *overwhelming majority* says climate change is going to destroy the Earth.

Cry wolf too often, and trust suffers.

The Big Apple

• • •

Nov. 9, 2015

For years I have had a love/hate relationship with The Big Apple, New York City. I lived there in the 1950s. My two sons were born there. For more years than I want to count, I have been a faithful reader of the *New Yorker* and the *New York Times*.

New York is the cultural and financial center of the world. The *New Yorker* magazine and the *New York Times* newspaper have long and ably represented that city.

My love affair with NYC began early when I visited with a high-school friend in the summer of 1944, before we both enlisted in the navy. We stayed at the YMCA in Manhattan and walked the streets with Midwest amazement at the rich East Coast metropolis.

In my college days I worked in a co-op job in a glamorous Times Square office. I spent my weekends and holidays walking all over the city, from Harlem to Greenwich Village to the Lower East Side, from Wall Street to Central Park to Washington Heights. Including the justly famous bridges to Brooklyn and Queens, not to mention the wonderful ferry you could take to Staten Island for a nickel in those early postwar days.

When my wife and I moved there after graduating from college in Ohio, I resumed my love affair with a city that had such cultural treasures—museums, theaters, diverse people of all colors and cultures, the incomparable Central Park, great music and art, and great universities. I took courses at Columbia and got my Masters degree in philosophy from New York University, while my wife studied painting on a scholarship at the Art Students League. I came close to a PhD (I did complete enough course work but could not afford the year off that a thesis would require). To get around, I loved the cheap, if noisy, subways (later I blamed them for my early-onset hearing loss, but that is another story).

Life was not a bed of roses in 1950s NYC. We lived paycheck to paycheck in poor neighborhoods of Manhattan. Often we had to get loans from pawnshops, especially after our sons were born. We had no health insurance but paid out of pocket the modest doctor's fees for both our sons' births (around two hundred dollars each).

Despite money and some depression problems, they were days of optimism. We had come out of World War II a winner, and the future looked bright. Thanks to the GI Bill, we had fine educations. Europe was in ruins, and most of the rest of the world was deep in poverty and disease, but we in the United States were on the upswing. We did have poverty and prejudice, but we also had a growing economy and optimism. We had never heard of the environment.

I was (and still am) a man of ideas, and the most important idea at that time was that we were privileged to live in the center of the greatest city of the greatest country in world history. I still think that, but since the 1950s, negatives have nearly eclipsed the positives. I have changed, and the city and the country have changed.

I went to college classes at Antioch with Coretta Scott (who later married Martin Luther King Jr.). I'm acutely aware that we owe a debt to the Civil Rights activists and Freedom Riders who, black and white, risked their lives to get rid of Jim Crow laws and customs in the fifties and sixties. I was sympathetic but regret now that I didn't play a more active role. Now that we have our first African American president, new progress in race relations is spotty. Many talented people of color have enjoyed great success in politics, education, business, sports, arts, and culture. Despite the Black is Beautiful movement of the sixties and today's Black Lives Matter, the plight of all too many average blacks remains grim. Recent wounds in Baltimore, Ferguson, and Chicago fester untreated.

I have long been a city walker. On many walks through many neighborhoods of 1950s NYC I don't recall that much fear, violence, or homelessness. This was also true of the many slum neighborhoods where we lived with people of color as neighbors. I'm not sure I could say the same if I walked the same walks today.

Sociology studies on the statistics of homelessness, poverty, crime, education, race, and violence in cities are confusing, conflicting, and not very trustworthy. As Charles Murray, libertarian political scientist and coauthor of *The Bell Curve*, writes, "The social sciences have been in the grip of a political orthodoxy that has had only the most tenuous connection with empirical reality, and too many social scientists think that threats to the orthodoxy should be suppressed by any means necessary. Corruption is the only word for it."[9]

Judging by my current reading in the *New Yorker* and the *New York Times*, I think Murray has a point. His "political orthodoxy" is what I call the left-liberal or Progressive-Green *clergy*. It's not a conspiracy, but a rough coalition of liberal educators, scientists, media stars, and politician has, for the most part, has ruled all of our cities (and to a somewhat lesser extent, our country and our Western world) for decades past.

This clergy has the best of intentions, with which I wholeheartedly agree. They favor tolerance, nonviolence, science, cooperation, peace, love, forgiveness, equality, justice, and prosperity. They are secular and not beholden to any otherworldly faith. (Some may be conventionally religious but don't blindly follow dogmas of any rigid or exclusive monotheistic faith—including Christianity.)

The clergy denies that the United States (or Western civilization or indeed the Modern Age) is exceptional. Instead, they tend to see Western culture as imperialist, racist, and corrupted by money and capitalism. Most of the clergy have little or nothing to say about Agricultural or Hunting/Gathering Ages. Many in the middle and upper classes are now taking up reactionary personal memes like tattoos, unusual body

---

9 Murray, Charles, "The Bell Curve 20 Years Later" (2014).

jewelry, rap music and culture, unwed parenthood, drugs, and four-letter vocabularies. (Come to think of it, most of these cultural habits actually come from longer ago—from the Hunting/Gathering Age!) Green enthusiasts seem eager to take us back to organic and natural trends also reminiscent of earlier ages, particularly the Agricultural one. All of these trends today get creative help from the *New Yorker* magazine and the *New York Times* newspaper.

The left-liberal Progressive-Green clergy are also suspicious of new technologies unless they are Green enough. They hate fossil fuels (but love to drive and fly). They predict catastrophe from climate change (in past decades it was overpopulation, resource scarcity, or DDT) but seldom take these predictions seriously enough to alter their personal lives. Most think democracy here should move toward European-style socialism. They imagine that big government can solve all our problems. A vocal minority wants people of color to take charge and thinks all will go better when white privilege ends.

This clergy is firmly in charge of New York City today. (The current mayor, Bill de Blasio, is a leader of both the Progressive and Green wings of the clergy.) This clergy is politically in firm control of most other major cities in the United States. Despite their good intentions, inequality and racial unrest are growing in all of them.

The *New Yorker* and the *New York Times* routinely publish articles, photos, fiction, and cartoons to promote these clergy views. Despite recent bizarre graphics, new viewing gimmicks (*Sunday New York Times* magazine), and good fiction (the *New Yorker*), both publications are losing readers rapidly and depend heavily on luxury ads from the richest percent and their trophy wives. If one of their stars, Hillary Clinton, does become the first female president, I predict the United States and Western civilization will suffer. Judging by the clergy's past record in big cities; women, Hispanics, and people of color will suffer the most.

Tidying up Loose Ends on the Clergy

• • •

Nov. 16, 2015

ONE LOOSE END IS THAT the clergy was near unanimous in praising the recent Hillary Clinton clash with Republicans investigating the Benghazi tragedy. The *New York Times* editorial said, "Unsurprisingly the hearing yielded no new information." They went on to lavishly praise her performance. The *New Yorker* did the same more smugly in its *Talk of the Town*.

"Don't believe those who say we learned nothing," reads a *Wall Street Journal* editorial. The editorial points out that Ms. Clinton (as well as UN ambassador Susan Rice and, by inference, Barack Obama) lied to us for political reasons—there was an upcoming election, and Obama had claimed al-Qaeda was on the skids. Clinton and Rice told us that the deaths of our ambassador and three aides were due to a "heinous and offensive video." At the same time, Hillary was telling the Egyptians (and presumably the president) the truth. The attack on 9/11 was in fact a well-planned al-Qaeda attack. (It happened on the tenth anniversary of the original attack, Sept. 11, 2011.) I remember her telling the same lie in a previous congressional hearing and shouting at legislators who objected, "What difference does it make?"

One difference is that lies like this for political gain do not make for a successful presidency.

Another loose end is the reality of the left-liberal clergy. Jane's son, Ravi, wrote in a past e-mail,

> Your characterization of college profs as 'clergy' sets them apart as a tribe…and renders them 'fodder for demonization.' Last week's *Big Apple* blog brought more doubt from Ravi. I think many of your so-called clergy are looking at the world through eyes and brains that are much like yours…I have been calibrating my bullshit meter my whole life, as I know you have. Perhaps editors at the *NYT* have bullshit meters too?…Your characterization of all the personnel at the *NYT* and others you view as liberals therefore sounds to me like a product of anger: simple, quick, sharp, hot, finger-pointing, jabbing, and demeaning…I do not see the world and other people this way, and I feel uncomfortable reading your words.

Ravi is right. I do get angry with the clergy, even though I know they have good intentions, and most of them are intelligent, able, and compassionate. Their bullshit meters must be defective, though. They don't seem to see that good intentions and compassion are necessary but not sufficient for progress.

I was once a member of that clergy myself. I taught tolerance, compassion, equality, freedom of religion, and faith in democracy, science, and technology. I taught Ravi. He was a good student, and I am delighted to see he still holds to these values as he calibrates his bullshit meter. When correctly calibrated, it should tell him that good intentions and compassionate values are fine but also can often pave the road to hell unless they are followed up by efficient and rationally grounded actions.

The recent news from the University of Missouri is a good example. I am sympathetic with the black (and the white) students who want the university to be more welcoming. I am even sympathetic with the obvious truth of "Black lives matter." I am not sympathetic with the activists' hunger strikes, threatening boycotts, making nonnegotiable demands, whining, and trampling on free speech and press.

The leaders, including some *clerical* professors, called for "muscle" to keep reporters from entering their campus tent city. They also led a chant: "Hey...ho...reporters have got to go." This is uncomfortably close to Jesse Jackson's chant in the sixties: "Hey...ho...Western civilization has got to go."

My guess is that it is no coincidence since politically correct attempts at race relations have much in common with totalitarian movements of the nineteenth and twentieth centuries: mob suppression of speech and press; shameless patronizing of racist and reactionary cultures; promotion of dependent victim-producing politically correct lifestyles; and bitter attacks on Western civilization claiming it to be imperialist, racist, technology obsessed, and capitalist led.

Why not try to be "more welcoming" instead?

At bottom, this is an attack on the Modern Age launched just little over 200 years ago by the United States and now being copied by most countries on Earth. The Modern Age has three things going for it—capitalism (which features private property, diverse talents, and free trade), science and technology, and freedom of and from religion. It came to its finest flower in democracies. It can exist in weakened and crippled form even in socialist or fascist states. It cannot exist in totalitarian ones, whether secular, Islamic, Buddhist, Hindu, Communist, Green-Progressive, or Christian.

In summary, many of the current US protests attack white privilege, Western civilization, and the Modern Age itself. Politically correct laws and regulations, mob action, patronizing welfare, and other reactionary memes encourage the protestors. Like Nazism, fascism, and communism, the protests are not only not progressive, but are deeply reactionary.

Among other facts they forget is that more than half a million privileged white men died in our Civil War to get rid of slavery, which had been a common practice everywhere on Earth for millennia past. They also forget that the very natural scarcity of land, gold, and slaves was the very reason why countries, tribes, and individuals in all previous ages needed and supported slavery, fought many savage wars, and committed horrendous crimes to get their fair share of resources which were what wealth amounted to in the Agricultural Age. And they forget that educated and smart white men, building on the European Enlightenment, launched a new country in 1776 that dramatically changed those ancient patterns. Slavery, serfdom, and peasantry were all soon abolished (yes, it did take sixty years, but compare that to the many tens of thousand years when it was common practice everywhere on Earth).

Capitalism, with its private property, free trade, diverse talents, and abundant profits, proved once and for all that it was not land or gold that made wealth but smart work for profit. It took a few hundred years and a couple of disastrous world wars to abolish Agricultural Age imperialism in the West. It still exists in abundance in the Agricultural Age Muslim world. Most non-Muslim nations today are convinced that it's better to live with some inequality than have socialist-style poverty be the norm for everyone.

In short, if you really want to end white privilege and substitute multiculturalism for Western civilization, you are likely to cripple the Modern Age. We can always return to a modern version of the Agricultural or the Hunting/Gathering Age, but it will likely be racist and totalitarian. You may also get slavery. serfdom, and peasantry, near-constant war, savage fights for fair shares, and severely reduced life spans for all.

Is it any wonder I get angry sometimes?

Intermission

● ● ●

OUR BED JUST MOVED DOWN one flight. Neither of us can easily manage a flight of stairs any more. I lie in bed in the morning and contemplate the spider crawling across the Victorian ceiling of what used to be our living room. Curious. Like most people today, we spend most of our *living* time in the kitchen or the bedroom.

That's not quite true. Jane and I do spend a good deal of time watching the news and then movies after supper in our other living room. Yesterday I saw on the news that Vladimir Putin was retaliating against the Western sanctions by banning food imports from the United States and the European Union countries. They showed a Moscow supermarket that I would never have recognized from my visit to Moscow in the late 1980s, when it was still the center of the Soviet Union. In those days under Leonid Brezhnev, supermarkets in Moscow were nonexistent. I once walked down a Moscow street and came upon a long line of people. A sign on a small grocery store gave a clue for the length of the line. It announced a new shipment of "oranges from Cuba." I could see some of the oranges through the dirty windows. They were scrawny.

Times have changed.

Fidel and I

• • •

Aug. 31, 2015

FIDEL CASTRO IS A MONTH older than I am. He has a beard. So do I. Fidel cares about the oppressed and downtrodden. So do I. Fidel is a confirmed socialist. I used to be a socialist, but I'm not anymore. Fidel is famous. I am not. Fidel led a major revolution in his home country. I figured out what the Modern Age of the world was all about.

Fidel is not in the best of moods now that our president has recognized his tyranny and stolen his excuse for the poverty of his country. Jane and I visited Cuba a few years ago, and it opened our eyes to the power and to the limits of socialism.

The power first:

We had a good time with the people of Cuba. Most citizens seemed relatively happy. We did not see any street demonstrations, riots, looting, or police brutality. We did not see any homeless people or beggars. Everyone, we were told, got free education and free health care. Everyone seemed to be well fed and all had shelter. Everyone was equal.

The limits:

Everyone was poor. The average—correction, the *only*—wage was sixteen dollars a month. Whether you operated on the brain or cleaned the operating-room floor didn't matter, you got sixteen dollars a month—the equivalent in pesos that is. Everyone wanted dollars, but you couldn't have any unless you got tips in the tourist trade or money from relatives in Florida. Cuba takes seriously the idea that all individuals should be equal in outcomes as well as opportunity. In Cuba, as in North Korea, they take this to the extreme. There is no such thing as private property. The government owns and controls everything: houses, apartments, offices, factories, businesses, food, land, sports, grocery stores, and organizations—literally everything.

Our cabdriver was a lawyer. He told us that he left the profession, as other professionals had, because he could make more money in tourist tips. He claimed that he worked harder and more effectively than other goof-off lawyers in his government office but got the same pittance salary. As a cabdriver, he was free now to work as hard as he liked and make more money in tips—and in dollars.

Many doctors and nurses do the same. Reading about health care in Cuba gives some pause. It is "free" and it scores high on international scorecards. But some reports show widespread shortages in doctors, nurses, drugs, and equipment, especially in rural areas. Mental health means lobotomy. Homosexual acts can land you in jail. (I understand that the treatment of gays and lesbians has improved since our visit.)

In Cuba, as in other socialist countries, there is a shortage of nearly everything. Even if you have money, there is little to spend it on. We visited groceries where food was very cheap. Typically they had ample rice and beans, *maybe* a few fruits and vegetables, or an occasional chicken. There were long lines for bread and no frozen or packaged food. Drugstores had no aspirin and not much else. Clothes and furniture stores were few and far between and, if found, had very limited merchandise. Automobiles, TV sets, cell phones, and computers were unavailable. The Internet was not available. I understand it still isn't. Education was free, but books and magazines were censored. Many were banned.

Housing was very cheap, often free. It left a lot to be desired, however. Here is the way a Havana writer, Pedro Juan Gutierrez, described his apartment:

> I went back to my room on the roof with its common bathroom, the most disgusting bathroom in the world, shared by fifty neighbors who multiply like rabbits since most of them are from the east of the island...They come to Havana in clumps, fleeing poverty...somehow they all live in a twelve-foot-square room...Each day no fewer than two hundred people shit, pee, and wash in that bathroom.[10]"

Behind the facades of decaying buildings lurks a world invisible to tourists. To learn about it, you have read *Dirty Havana Trilogy*, by Pedro Juan Gutierrez; *Against All Hope: The Prison Memoirs of Armando Valladares*; *Commies: A Journey through the Old Left, the New Leaf, and the Leftover Left*, by ex-communist Ronald Radosh; or *Ay, Cuba* by public radio host Andrei Codrescu.

Reading, you will discover a dark world of bitter poverty; mothers, daughters, and sons in prostitution to make a few dollars; abortion as birth control; dissidents in prison; and a proud people longing for freedom and often willing to risk their lives to get to freedom in Florida. You can observe as we did: an almost total lack of maintenance; employees goofing off; gross inefficiency; rude salesclerks; corruption and pollution everywhere (along with a few organic gardens for show).

Codrescu finishes his book,

> This is your truth. Fidel is a saint now...He is serene. He is negotiating with European capitalists, but in his heart of hearts he'd rather negotiate with Disney [probably now his brother Raúl is!]. Only Disney, you see, could keep Cuba both socialist and capitalist by declaring it Commieland, a place where the workers of the world can see the dream in action—and on vacation. Fidel will die a saint. Ay, Cuba. [11]

---

10 Gutierrez, Pedro Juan, *Dirty Havana Trilogy* (2002).
11 Codrescu, Andrei, *Ay, Cuba* (1999).

How can we profit from our new relationship? We can both learn. Cuba can learn the power of freedom to make an economy grow. We can learn some benefits of social justice.

To escape poverty, Cuba needs the power of free-market capitalism. They will have to allow for some inequality for this to happen, as both China and India have discovered after decades of disastrous experiments with equality of outcomes.

The United States needs to have more economic growth and more minority wealth. Somehow, someway, we need to marry libertarian freedom with social justice, so that our country can lead in future Modern Ages as we have in past.

How to do this is *the* challenge of our times.

Try a Little Kindness

● ● ●

Feb. 8, 2016

I GOT STUCK IN THE snow last week in my driveway trying to get out and go to the VA hospital here in Madison for minor surgery on my nose for skin cancer. A young man, a stranger to me, came along and kindly helped me out. At the hospital, taking the skin cancer from my nose was a success but a bit painful. I much appreciated the elderly nurse who kindly squeezed my hand while the doctors cut. These are the sorts of things that happen to me often lately.

For instance, a few weeks before, I was taking Frankie for a short walk and unwisely stepped on a patch of snow and fell awkwardly in the street. I had trouble getting up. Once again, a couple of nice, young, good-looking women joggers came to my assistance and helped me up. It's the sort of thing that happens often lately.

I'm not sure whether I have just been lucky or I live in a city full of kind people or just that I am getting old, but I am happy to report these kind deeds with so many cruel ones so common in the news.

Come to think about it, I'm not sure Madison is that special. Jane and I have traveled widely in many cities, states, and countries and have consistently been impressed by the kindness shown to strangers. Whether it was Bamako, Mali, where we played golf with friendly caddies at the only golf course in the country (built by the Chinese!); Kunming, China, where we danced in the street with many friendly and exuberant Chinese; Berlin, Germany, where we stayed in a friendly pension apartment and met an old friend at Checkpoint Charlie who we had no idea was in Germany; Osaka, Japan, where we stayed with a nice family who dressed us both in traditional kimonos for a picture. (The husband was retired from Hitachi and was a golfer but confessed that playing in Japan was "kind of expensive." Instead he flew often to Guam or Hawaii to golf because it was cheaper!)

Or Budapest, Hungary, where we were entertained in a plush apartment overlooking the Danube at the thousandth anniversary of the city's founding and saw the most dramatic display of fireworks (given by Japan) that I have ever seen; Port au Prince, Haiti, where we had some friendly "ball boys" when we were playing tennis at a diplomatic residence compound (in partial payment for their efficient and friendly help, we in turn gave them some tennis rackets and balls); in England, Scotland, and Ireland, where we stayed in the nicest B&Bs ever and had the best meals that I can remember anywhere; Dayton, Ohio, where I grew up and still feel welcome when I visit; Denver, Colorado, where some of Jane's children live and work and often come to Wisconsin to help us; Baltimore, Maryland and Titusville, Florida, where my two sons live and work and often come to Wisconsin to help us; and vice versa, we visit the children and families to help them (we used to that is—sadly it's getting hard to travel much now).

On all of our many trips, statewide and foreign, we often came across kind waitresses who sat with us in booths and helped us read the menu; motel guests who helped us make the free waffles for breakfast; motel clerks who let us use the pool and hot tub after hours; and the many, many kind people who unfailingly went way out of their way in all countries, states, and cities to give us directions when we got lost, which was often.

In short, polite consideration has been the rule in our lives, not the exception. More often than not, it has been accompanied by the amazing kindness of strangers. I give thanks to all of them, including my readers many of whom are also strangers to me.

Where am I going with this?

It doesn't make for very exciting movies, fiction, or nightly news, but we have found that kindness between people—one on one—is actually more common than bluster or bombast, arrogance, violence and crime.

It's just good to know.

Pope Francis

● ● ●

Oct. 5, 2015

IT IS TOUGH TO CRITICIZE Pope Francis. The pope is an attractive, humble man. He calls for more love and forgiveness in this rough world. Who can disagree? He tugs on our heartstrings when he hugs handicapped children and shakes hands with tattooed, thuggish prisoners. He drives a Fiat, not a Mercedes or Cadillac. He comes from neighboring South America, not from an ocean-apart Europe.

I hate to point out that, despite his charm, the seventy-eight-year-old pope is a hopeless reactionary. His calls for more love and forgiveness as well as his personal humility seem sincere enough. But my guess is his deeper desire is to reverse the Modern Age and nudge us back to medieval times. (Many of his best friends here, Progressives and Greens in the Democratic Party, may well share that desire, but are even more unaware of it.)

For Pope Francis, as for many Greens and Progressives, the good old days were not that bad. The papacy (and the clergy) was supreme; science was "settled" (as it was before Copernicus and Galileo, and as the Green-Progressives claim it is today); God and his church called all the shots (translation: today the *clergy* of professors, media stars, and government bureaucrats set the tone and call the shots today); charity (social welfare programs today) is the answer to poverty (plus calls for diversity, more charity from the rich, and still more *clergy*—translation, more young people in college) are the answer to economic woes;

competition, inequality, and capitalist profits are the evil and above all, all decent citizens should "significantly limit their consumption" to assure sustainability, help the poor (wealth and resources are like a big pie and the governmental clergy should decide who gets how big a piece in the division); and we should not let the Earth "look more and more like an immense pile of filth." (Unsettling reminder: the medieval days were infamous for rampant pollution, deadly famines, lavish lords' and ladies' extravagant lifestyles, and frequent deadly plagues.)

All of that Catholic Christian dogma is not shared with his left-liberal friends but still is dogma for a Catholic Christian like the Pope: that women should stay in their place as nuns, wives, mothers, mistresses, or prostitutes; that gay or lesbian life is a no-no; birth control, abortion, and sodomy are even stricter no-no's; and above all, salvation of souls is the overriding goal in life while hell is the eternal punishment for the unsaved.

Tellingly in his trip to the United States the pope did not dwell on these dogmas—"who am I to judge?" (He also kept quiet his secret meeting with the Kentucky Christian clerk who had refused a gay marriage license.)

Pope Francis took his name from a popular Italian saint, and he is the first Jesuit pope. Jesuits have traditionally *manned* the front lines of the Catholic Church in combating heresies and in missionary efforts to save souls in Asia, Africa, and Native America. Now that supernatural and exclusive monogamous religious beliefs are fading in the West, any potential for growth is now in poor locations like Cuba, Africa, and South America, where the pope is a frequent visitor (with accompanying high carbon footprints).

Pope Francis is from Argentina, a country that used to be a leader in Modern Age wealth creation and living standards but has been in steep decline for decades. According to the business journal *Barron's*, "it has been plagued by the enduring example of Juan Perón and his state-managed capitalism as much as by military dictators and left-wing revolutionaries. Its corrupt leaders have nationalized businesses, defaulted on debt, and promoted inflation. Argentinian capitalism is an insult to capitalism."

We had another important foreign visitor recently, President Xi Jinping of China. He was not as popular or as publicized as the pope. So far as I know, Xi didn't visit any prisons or bless any handicapped children or prisoners, but he could have given lessons to Pope Francis on how to help people out of poverty. Contrary to popular and papal opinion, according to the United Nations, "extreme poverty hasn't doubled or remained the same. It has fallen from 35% in 1994 to 14% in 2011." China is responsible for most of this decrease. And without question, China's progress is due to its abandonment of Marxist socialism and its embrace of free markets, private property, diverse talents, and free trade—old-fashioned capitalism straight out of Adam Smith's *Wealth of Nations*.

One result is that we are now in serious economic competition with China and not with the Vatican. Once we were in competition with the Vatican. In 1776, Catholics were widely considered to be the Antichrist. In fact, our Founding Fathers were suspicious of any and all exclusive religions like Catholicism, Islam, and Judaism. Judeo-Christian Protestants did influence them, but the secular Enlightenment influenced them more. The Founding Fathers declined to commit the new nation to any religion. To enforce this unique prohibition, they wrote into the Constitution a specific amendment to assure freedom *of* religion, which included the equally important freedom *from* religion. (Jefferson was accused often of atheism, Thomas Paine was an open atheist AND Benjamin Franklin was a Freemason for all of his long life.)

Xi and his immediate predecessors changed China for the better much more than did their socialist hero, Chairman Mao Zedong. Mao was like Mahatma Gandhi of India—charismatic, popular, and renowned if not worshiped as an international celebrity. Both Mao and Gandhi promoted different versions of a secular Christian heresy, socialism/communism. It was sold as (and still is) a shortcut to abolish poverty and create a healthier community. It has failed time and time again to do so.

Mao preached peasant virtues but massacred intellectuals and starved millions of peasants in government-caused famines. Gandhi preached Hindu nonviolence, independence, religious and caste tolerance, and local organic production. Unfortunately, with the best of intentions, he brought nearly a half-century of poverty, pollution, and violence to both Hindus and Muslims. The not-nearly-as-well-known governing successors of both Mao and Gandhi realized that you must create wealth before redistributing it. Both China and India are conquering poverty now not by compassionate aid, missionary zeal, or foreign charity but by using market methods, condemned now by the pope and most radical Green-Progressives in the Western world.

If we were to really follow Pope Francis and the radical Progressive-Green Democrats, we, too, could end up an Agricultural Age kingdoms like Cuba, North Korea, Venezuela, Middle Eastern and North African Islamic states and the former Soviet bloc countries. Alas with accompanying poverty, government domination, rank pollution, frequent epidemics, famines, and severely shortened life spans. I compensation, we would have prayer, love, forgiveness, and charity. True, that many countries in modern Europe seem to have escaped that dismal fate with a milder form of socialism. They too are beginning to suffer from these same maladies. It takes time.

Broken Bones and Medicare

• • •

March 10, 2014

MODERN HEALTH CARE IN AMERICA is fiendishly complex, surprisingly good, and very expensive. A personal story has made it more real.

Jane and I have taken extra precautions this icy winter when we go walking with Frankie, our dog. Wouldn't you know, last Thursday evening Jane fell in our ice-free kitchen and fractured her hip.

I had to call 911 for a city ambulance. To the city's credit, three husky paramedics from the fire department arrived promptly and carried Jane in blankets to the emergency room at Meriter Hospital.

The doctors and nurses at Meriter hospital managed the pain and surgically mended her hip with impressive skill and dispatch. Her family doctor told me that operating on a ninety-year-old woman was indeed risky, but the alternative was for her to spend the rest of her life with bedsores in a nursing home. The surgery went fine, and she is recovering nicely. Tuesday she went to a skilled nursing home for rehab, and within a few weeks, I have every confidence she will be home on Gilman Street, and things will be back to normal.

I go into some detail describing this misfortune to point out that we have good health care in this country. (Or at least we do in Madison. My former wife, Virginia, reported that she had to wait eight hours to get treatment in Tucson, Arizona.) As far as I am aware, the same care Jane got here would have been given to anyone in Madison, whether they could pay or not.

But *somebody* has to pay.

We signed up two years ago with a Medicare Advantage Plan (Humana) because it was easier to get drug benefits (Part D of Medicare). I knew that Humana was a private company and wanted to make a profit. Up until now they have done a fine job for us, and I have no complaints. We have received all of the benefits Medicare would offer along with prescription drug payments. I assume Humana has made a profit. The losers are younger taxpayers who paid for these benefits.

With the coming of the Affordable Care Act (Obamacare), all of the Advantage Plans have had to change, too. To maintain their profitability, they, too, have had to make health care more affordable. As is now happening with both Medicare and Medicaid, this means reducing costs and/or raising copays is one answer. One way to reduce costs is to restrict the "network" of providers—hospitals, nursing homes, doctors, and so forth—to those that the company (or the government) can make good deals with. Just a year and a half ago, Jane went to a nice rehab facility for her new knee, a facility no longer on the Humana network. This time with her damaged hip, we had to search far and wide for one that would take Humana patients.

That good health care Jane received was expensive, not only because of the highly paid anesthesiologist and surgeon, high-tech equipment, and lab technicians, but also the luxurious room and meals, the nurses, and nurse assistants—not even to mention the parking lot attendants, the lunchroom cashiers, the janitors, valet parkers, and the first-class building itself with spotless corridors, express elevators, and luxurious private rooms. None of this comes cheap. My son-in-law Samuel, who has lived for years in Europe, tells me that hospitals and clinics there are not nearly as luxurious as ours.

It will change, but today most hospitals, doctors, and skilled nursing facilities in this country routinely take Medicare and Medicaid patients at little or no cost to the patient. The government pays, though—over three thousand dollars a day for skilled nursing home care, and that's just for room and board. Physical and occupational therapies are extra. Hospital care of course, not to mention emergency room care, is much more. Our Humana plan used to pay the whole bill but now requires us to copay twenty-five dollars a day for the first twenty days and $150/day for days after twenty. Emergency room care is still more expensive.

Some would say Humana is making a profit, so why shouldn't they suck up the extra costs now? Being a good capitalist, I think this view is shortsighted. Profits are in great measure responsible for the superior health care we now have.

On a personal level, like most people, I am on the lookout for a better bargain, so I tried to investigate and compare our Medicare Advantage Plan to straight Medicare (where the government pays the total nursing home bill—at least for now). To get the prescription help (Part D), you have to contract with a private company. I can sympathize with the hapless citizens trying to sign up for Obamacare and having to cope with website malfunctions and incredibly complex choices. In trying to compare the respective advantages of Medicare (A, B, & D) and Medicare Advantage Plans (Part C—like Humana, United Health, or Blue Cross), you are asked hundreds of questions. You try your best to answer them, and you end up crashing your computer and never even getting to the "choices." I have an above-average computer and Internet connection, as well as above-average intelligence and education. For the below-average or even average computers, Internet connections, and intelligence—50 percent of the population—it must be well nigh impossible.

If you are holding your breath for my solution, don't. I don't have any. I wish I did. I don't like the government controlling such an important and large segment of our economy. And, as longtime readers are aware, I have grave questions about the efficiency of government help programs, especially ones as complex as health care.

Up until now, private health insurance with profits has led the way to a surprisingly good health care system. I do think government aid is needed for basic research and for the elderly and for the poor (Medicare and Medicaid). We have that now. But will mandating—and controlling—private insurance for everyone lead to better health care for everyone?

Don't count on it.

Odd Couples

● ● ●

May 9, 2016

STIPULATION: I AM NOT RACIST. When I write about groups I do not mean or imply that *all* members of *any* group are alike. I agree totally and enthusiastically with Martin Luther King Jr. that one should judge *individuals* on their characters and not on their membership in groups. One of the beauties of the Modern Age (founded by the United States in 1776) is diversity—diversity in opportunity, talent, race, religion, sexual orientation, knowledge, culture, and economic contribution. When I say Jews and blacks are an odd couple due to vast differences in wealth and achievement between them, it may be offensive to many but it is what it is. I do *not* mean *all* Jews or *all* blacks.

Did you ever admire someone don't know much about—scientist, writer, artist, composer, actor, business leader, or whatever? For me, nine out of ten he or she has turned out to be a Jew or in the more politically correct adjective—Jewish. Only rarely has he or she turned out to be black or in the more PC term—African American. While this is true for me, I recognize and respect that it may not be true for people more devoted to sports, politics, or popular music than I am, or not as devoted to ideas as I am. (Note: I do admire President Obama.)

Jews have been very successful in America. Blacks have not. That seems to be changing today in politics, music, and sports, but not that much in wealth and intellectual achievement. Jews, for instance, make up only 0.02 percent of the world but have won 129 Nobel Prizes. By contrast, Muslims, 22 percent of the world, and have won four. Non-Jewish people of color, the vast majority of the world's population, have won only fifteen—one for economics, two for literature, and twelve for peace.

As for wealth, Bernie Sanders rails against Wall Street but never mentions that 140 of the *Forbes* four hundred rankings of richest Americans (35 percent) are Jews like Bernie. He also doesn't talk much about his own income. According to his 2015 tax return, Bernie pulls in over $200 thousand a year, considerably more than the average bloke. He also takes more deductions than average, reducing his tax rate to 13.4 percent, significantly lower than that most workers must pay. As Donald Trump might say, "Bernie is smart."

The *New Yorker* magazine is one of the most important publishers of quality fiction, nonfiction, poetry, and art. I checked on the recent spring 2016 issue and found that Jews wrote all (100 percent) of it. Even the artist from Argentina who did the cover was Jewish! I realize Jews make up a larger proportion of the NYC population (8 percent) than in the country as a whole (2 percent). But I can't help wondering why the *New Yorker* could not find a few black or non-Jewish writers of quality. (I do note that they have recently added two black writers to their staff, and on occasion I'm aware that they do publish non-Jewish white writers of quality like John Updike.)

I haven't checked the *New York Times* or other liberal—and not so liberal—newspapers and magazines (or books), but my guess is that the proportions are similar. A Jewish family owns the *New York Times* and most of the editors, reporters, and columnists, are Jewish. This extreme disproportion in publishing is true in many other fields of intellectual achievement, wealth, and power.

Los Angeles; Washington, DC; and New York City are all famous for outstandingly successful Jews in the media, entertainment, and political arenas while blacks and non-Jewish whites are grossly underrepresented. (Correction: recently that may not be true of blacks at some levels. I could be wrong, but judging by what I read and see in modern TV and print ads, sports, entertainment, music, and some of the other arts black people may actually be a little *overrepresented* today. One can't be certain, but a patronizing boost from Jewish owners and the unseen and unacknowledged power of bell curves on talent are the most likely causes.)

Jews and blacks are *not* an odd couple when it comes to fierce commitment to social justice. Understandably, they also share fierce resentment for past injustice. Anti-Semitism originated in Christian Europe's Agricultural Age and in the twentieth century it led to genocide in Germany's Holocaust. Anti-black prejudice originated in all civilizations of the Agricultural Age and led to the Modern Age to the horrors of slavery, Jim Crow, lynching, and vicious bigotry. Both Jews and Blacks have ample motives to lead and support modern secular Christian heresies like socialism, communism, and many other protest movements.

Are these wide gaps in wealth and achievement due to heredity or culture? Are Jews simply smarter, or is their culture more suited to success in the idea-prone Modern Age achievement world?

On the culture side, Jews have traditionally urged their children to work hard, get good educations, and go all out to be successful in business, professions, sciences, and arts. Black parents have, for the most part, failed in these same tasks. That failure may be understandable considering their history of slavery, poverty, and prejudice and the fact that current welfare doesn't help. Regardless of causes—it is what it is.

It is worth noting that after the great migration of Jews to the United States from Russia and Eastern Europe in the early twentieth century, scientists labeled Jewish immigrants as *below average* in IQ. Current science on the other hand shows Jewish children with *above-average* IQs and black children with below-average IQs!

What can be done to improve on these gross inequalities? It's like the old joke, "How can you be successful in the restaurant business?" Answer: "It's easy. All you have to do is think of a way."

One way I suggest is to expand social security payments to *all* citizens, not just the old or disabled. All of us are disabled in one form or another. We could pay for this expensive expansion by eliminating most of the charitable *help* from the government that really does not help. Instead it encourages dependency, drugs, and crime and does little to produce education, achievement, and wealth. A national basic income might help to bring about the opposite—encourage education, achievement, and wealth—and for all citizens, not just Jews and blacks.

This idea may be simplistic and impossible now. In the long run, I think it will be inevitable.

Bah Humbug! (In Defense of Scrooge, Potter, and Steve Jobs)

• • •

Dec. 23, 2013

"BAH HUMBUG!" WAS ALL EBENEZER Scrooge could say about Christmas. Henry Potter, the rich banker and slumlord in the movie *It's a Wonderful Life*, was equally gloomy about Christmas cheer. I'm not sure what the real-life Steve Jobs thought about Christmas, but Jobs, too, was a shrewd businessman not known for humanitarian gestures.

All three are examples of capitalism in action. And all three are misleading.

Charles Dickens (himself a bit of a racist) first thought of the character Scrooge for his novel *A Christmas Carol* when he was walking in a Scottish cemetery and came upon the tombstone of Ebenezer Lennox Scroogle, a relative of the famous capitalism sage, Adam Smith (who knows, perhaps a relative of mine, since my great-grandmother was from the Lennox clan in Scotland). The tombstone identified Scroogle as a "meal man" (corn merchant). Dickens misread this as a "mean man" and wrote in his diary that it must have "shriveled" Scroogle's soul to carry "such a terrible thing to eternity."

Scrooge in Dickens's *A Christmas Carol* was indeed a mean man. He thought giving employees paid holidays is "just an excuse for picking my pocket." As a boss, though, his stinginess may have been of more benefit in the long run to low-wage workers like Bob Cratchit than any gifts he gives than any raises and gifts he might give in the present that make him such a sweetie.

Protestors today have similar complaints about low wages at McDonald's, Wal-Mart, and other restaurants and stores. Politicians routinely suggest raising the minimum wage. The motive is good; the unplanned results are not. Raising the minimum wage encourages more automation; sends more jobs to China and Mexico; increases illegal immigration; makes it harder for young, low-skilled, and low-IQ citizens to get a foothold on the economic ladder; increases unemployment; helps unions raise wages and bankrupt more cities like Detroit; encourages crime; and in the long run stuffs our already overflowing prisons.

If you're going to flout the laws of supply and demand, why not raise the minimum to fifty dollars an hour or for that matter, a hundred dollars an hour? Merchants can raise the prices on hamburgers, fries, organic foods, pharmaceutical drugs, recycling services, and iPhones to equally ridiculous figures, and soon we will need a bushel basket of cash to bring Christmas cheer to anyone. Alternatively, you could nationalize the whole economy, as Cuba does, and give everyone an identical wage as Cuba does. Or you could return to a medieval state, where lord-like bureaucrats, instead of the market, could decide what citizens should get. My common sense tells me the best solution is not to raise the minimum wage at all, but to abolish it.

The rich plutocrat banker Henry Potter in *It's a Wonderful Life* has also been widely condemned. Potter, like Scrooge, may be personally stingy, mean, and even a bit of a thief, but in the long run, Potter's banking creed is more likely to benefit people than the softhearted "bleeding heart" one of George Bailey.

Remember the plot. Rich Henry Potter (Lionel Barrymore) sets out to destroy a small savings and loan company run by George Bailey (Jimmy Stewart). Bailey is known for his good deeds. He stops a run on his bank with his meager personal cash, but his savings and loan almost collapses when his Uncle Billy makes a foolish mistake, and Potter takes advantage.

After an entertaining series of plot turns, including the intercession of a guardian angel when George tries to kill himself, George triumphs in the end. Friends and relatives come through with lots of fungible Christmas cheer—cash, that is. As the narrator says, while the audience—including me—shed tears of holiday joy and a wise narrator says, "Remember, no man is a failure if he has friends."

The most plausible scenario I have read to explain the housing bubble that burst in 2008 and caused such devastation to the worldwide economy is that it was due not to lack of regulation of Wall Street—but too much regulation by the government.

Years earlier (under both Democratic and Republican rule) Congress, like George Bailey, wanted to make it more affordable to own a home. They nudged banks and, when that didn't work well enough, *forced* them under threat of losing their licenses to make a slew of risky loans with low or no down payments, and never mind about credit histories. These well-intentioned laws were meant to help the working poor, especially minorities.

The new laws had unplanned and unpleasant side effects. Many middle-class and rich people found that they, too, could take advantage of new "affordable" terms to buy bigger houses or to refinance and use the equity to live more lavishly. Home prices (rentals, too) for rich and for the poor soared, we had a huge housing bubble, and soon we had an equally huge backlog of bad loans. Like the current Affordable Care Act and the pension crises in Detroit and many other cities and states, including Puerto Rico now and many foreign states like Greece, Italy, France, and Spain), the government had created a monster that was unsustainable. We still haven't completely recovered from the fallout.

I realize there are counterarguments. If you can stand the invective, see *Daily Kos* for some. Their main argument seems to be generic: "it's all a pack of lies."

And then we come to Steve Jobs. Unlike the fictional Scrooge and Potter, Steve was popular, even more so after his early death at fifty-six from pancreatic cancer. He was a brilliant innovator, a creative marketer, and a capitalist without peer. Like many rich capitalists his work benefited the world, but his ruthless pattern of business success was similar to the fictional villains Potter and Scrooge. His angry denunciation and domination of subordinates and suppliers (superiors, too) was legendary. He paid his Chinese assembly workers less than Bob Cratchit and worked them longer hours. Steve also went to extreme lengths to enforce secrecy. He once sued a thirteen-year-old blogger who dared to publish speculation about a new product.

Yet he remained a media and leftist darling. So it goes.

Intermission

● ● ●

IT IS A SOBERING EXPERIENCE to surf through the two-hundred-plus channels of your cable TV contract. Who watches all this stuff?

Like most people, I have a few favorites—CNN, Fox News, MSNBC, PBS, TCM (Turner Classic Movies—with no commercials), and whatever sports channel is covering my favorite Wisconsin teams. All this constitutes only a minuscule percentage of what my cable company makes available, and I pay for. Besides the foreign-language and the all-music channels that I never watch or listen to, there are hundreds, nay thousands, of movie, sports, business, education, game-show, science, soap-opera, history, mystery, and ad-sponsored opportunities for entertainment and learning that I have zero interest in watching.

The Below Average

• • •

Feb. 24, 2014

Last week I quoted from Garrison Keillor's mythical Lake Woebegone, where "all the men are good looking, all the women are strong, and all the children are above average." It is a charming fantasy. What about the real world, where 50 percent of the men, women, and children are by definition below average?

The Civil Rights revolution of the sixties was long overdue. It helped not only African Americans but opened the doors of opportunity for women, Latinos, other minorities, and is doing so now for LBGT people. We can see the results today in the very large increase of women and minorities in positions of power and wealth, many in the top 5 percent—way above average.

An unintended result of other sixties- and New Deal–inspired programs in the "war on poverty" was a huge increase in below-average blacks and below-average whites in prison. In 1950 when I graduated from college, we had a population of around 125 million and a prison population of around twenty-five thousand, roughly one in five thousand. By 2000, the US population had doubled, but the prison population had jumped eight times to more than two million—one out of every 125. Blacks today are imprisoned fifteen times as much as they were in 1950; whites too are imprisoned five times as much. While the above-average black and the above-average white have done well, the below-average black or white, and their *below-average* children have not.

Much of this is due to the government's destructive family policies—especially the toxic combination of minimum-wage laws and aid to dependent children. The unintended result of these compassionate programs was a closing of the opportunity doors to the below average, and unlike Lake Woebegone this means 50 percent of the population. Young men and women of below-average talents, black or white, are now suffering from super high unemployment rates in America. Unemployment rates are even higher in the United Kingdom and other social-welfare democracies in Europe. The number of children with no father has also skyrocketed.

So what can be done?

Our economic system today is so efficient and productive that we actually don't need as many unskilled, low-ability, and below-average workers as we did in Agricultural Age. We may not even need as many middle-class bureaucrats! In those days, the below average and the middle-class *average* worker could always find work on the farm or in the factory. Even in the transition time of the early Modern Age—the nineteenth and early twentieth centuries—the below average could still be farm helpers or low-level factory workers, and their work there was vital to the economy. Today, farm workers make up only 2 percent of the population and are declining as I write. Agriculture, manufacturing, and mining output have more than doubled in output since my youth but with many fewer workers. These jobs have been lost mostly not to China, Mexico, or any other developing country but to automation.

One result of this ever-increasing wealth of goods and services is an ever-declining need for unskilled labor. It leaves us with three choices: (1) let the below average, *or the average*, go jobless and be homeless and hungry; (2) continue our present social-welfare expansion with ever-larger increases in cost, dependency, crime, prison populations, government bureaucracy, high taxes, and immigration problems; or (3) try some version of a guaranteed national income for all.

I vote for the third choice. Suppose we were to scrap most of the anti-poverty, education, environmental, crony subsidy, and wealth-transfer programs (which are presently costing trillions of dollars a year) and instead simply give social security checks to all citizens—and I do mean *all*. No discrimination by need, age, race, wealth, sexual orientation, or religion.

Just as important, we don't tax that basic income.

Believe it or not, we could do this using the revenue presently being spent for antipoverty programs, food stamps, aid to dependent children, subsidies to crony-capitalist corporations and nonprofit groups, federal pensions, federal health care and education subsidies, useless and downright harmful environmental regulations, and the like. The big difference would be that 311 million of us would make the decisions where to spend the money instead of a few thousand government planners and bureaucrats.

The basic-income payment would be enough to live a modest middle-class lifestyle, but not enough for much luxury. Most people would want to pursue happiness at a grander level and increase that base income by working. These people—they would be the majority of both the above average, the average, and the below average (we do need some unskilled workers)—would get satisfying and productive jobs. The basic income grant would not be taxed, but additional income from a job would be. Most government revenue, as it does today, would come from these *working* folks.

This kind of social security program could at a stroke abolish poverty; encourage marriage, families, and wanted children; decrease prison populations; increase win-win transactions and economic growth; decrease zero-sum jobs in government and elsewhere; decrease losses from crony capitalism, inefficiency, and harmful overregulation; open up opportunities for all classes; and make moot most concerns about inequality, minimum wage, unemployment, abortion, sexual discrimination, and many other education and health care issues.

I realize this won't happen tomorrow or "at a stroke." Our federal system offers hope, though. Colorado has just passed laws legalizing marijuana. Maybe some brave governor and progressive state can pioneer a guaranteed income for residents and we can see how it works.

Such a strategy could also offer the promise of some bipartisan cooperation. Republican conservatives and libertarians, who want more freedom and opportunity, could join hands with left-liberal Democrats, who want to spend more for the needy and increase demand for the economy. John Maynard Keynes, the liberal economist the Democrats like to follow, once wrote an article called "Economic Possibilities for Our Grandchildren." In it he suggests, "Civilization might one day settle on a 15-hour workweek, with three hours of daily labor being sufficient to satisfy the old Adam in most of us."

Jeepers! That's about what I work now. Let's give it a try.

Stimmig

• • •

Dec. 2, 2013

ONE OF FRANKLIN ROOSEVELT'S MAIN advisers was Stuart Chase. He was a socialist economist from the Massachusetts Institute of Technology who is given credit for coining the term *New Deal*. After his visit to the new Soviet Union in 1927, Chase wrote, "Sixteen men in Moscow today are attempting one of the most audacious economic experiments in human history...They are laying down the industrial future of 146 million people...These sixteen men salt down the whole economic life of 146 million people for a year in advance as calmly as a Gloucester man salts down his fish."

Chase finished his influential book, *The New Deal*, with the question, "Why should Russians have all the fun remaking a world?"

Obama and the Democrats are following the New Deal example, hoping to remake the economic and social life of the United States. They are also following the lead of social-welfare democracies in Europe, which are trying the same trick.

Last week I claimed that movies like *Hunger Games* and *Avatar* were weapons in a second Cold War on the Modern Age. The Modern Age is founded on progress on three fronts: science and technology, free-market capitalism, and freedom of and *from* religion (notably the Christian versions). I concluded, "Instead of trying to copy European social welfare democracies, we might do better with a *stimmig* approach now being considered in both rich Switzerland and poor Cyprus."

Like the popular German word *Schadenfreude*, there is no exact equivalent in English for *stimmig*. Annie Lawrey in the *New York Times Magazine* wrote that *stimmig* means "'coherent and harmonious' with a dash of 'beauty' thrown in."

The basic idea behind stimmig is that the poor are poor because they don't have enough money. So give them money. A German-born artist, Enno Schmidt, leads a basic-income movement in Switzerland that wants the government to provide just that, a guaranteed annual income to all Swiss citizens. Activists in Cyprus are pushing the same idea. It is similar to a scheme proposed in this country by libertarian political scientist Charles Murray in his book, *In Our Hands: A Plan to Replace the Welfare State*.

Let's say we send a check for a thousand dollars a month to everyone in the United States, no strings attached. This would mean a family of four would have a basic income of forty-eight thousand dollars a year without working. This is slightly below the median family income today but much higher than the poverty level. Ergo, every family becomes middle class, at least economically.

There are around 313 million of us in the country, so we would need a little less than four trillion dollars a year to do that. It turns out that this is roughly what federal, state, and local governments are spending today for health care, education, food stamps, pensions, antipoverty programs, unemployment insurance, crony-capitalist subsidies, and the like. Why not give that money directly to the citizens and let them decide what to do with it, instead of letting government bureaucrats make all the decisions?

Automation and global competition have left us with an economy where we don't have (or need) all the jobs as we did just fifty years ago. Manufacturing output in this country, for instance, has more than doubled since 1972, even though we have many fewer jobs in our factories. Even middle-class managers are having trouble finding jobs. In other words, we already are creating enough wealth in this country to expand social security to the young as well as the old and the disabled. If we make the payments in cash instead of services, we would have millions of individuals making decisions about their own education, health care, food, shelter, and the like. In effect, this will give every individual the same opportunities the rich have today when they send their children to private schools, pay for excellent health care, and provide their children with million-dollar trust funds.

Consider the advantages. We would finally win the war on poverty. We would empower citizens to make choices about their own health care, education, food, housing, and retirement (as they did before the New Deal came along in the 1930s). We would break the cycle of dependence, single parenthood, drugs, crime, and prisons presently fostered by big-government charity programs. We could stop worrying about unemployment problems and jobs going to Mexico or China.

True, some would take advantage and not work but spend the free money on wine, women, and song—and drugs. That's what some do today on need-based welfare, and some of the rich have always done. We would still have religious and secular charity to take care of the extreme exceptions. I'm betting that most citizens would behave like most middle-class people do today—work, save, and have the ambition to do more with their own life, liberty, and pursuit of happiness.

With stimmig, we wouldn't need to fuss and argue about minimum-wage laws or unemployment benefits. We would encourage marriage, family life, the arts, and sciences. We would get more sports and leisure. Paradoxically, we would foster responsibility and discourage crime. With less crime, we would have fewer people in prisons and many fewer homeless people. We would bypass contentious issues like birth control, abortion, and inequality in education and wealth. We would have more freedom, and lastly, we would need many many fewer government employees, many of them hopelessly inefficient at present (note the Obama Care website fiasco).

Vouchers for food, housing, education, or health care are a step in the right direction, but a guaranteed annual income would be better. Cash is fungible. Let the people decide what they want to spend it on. As for the few who would take advantage and squander it, so be it. Many squander billions now in our present social welfare systems.

Government employees and unions, crony capitalists, sustainable Greens, trial lawyers, business lobbyists, social workers, and all the other groups that flourish today virtue of government monopolies might not like it. So? They are not the ones responsible for crucial things that support and advance the Modern Age: (1) science and technology, (2) free-market capitalism, and (3) Christian-derived compassion, justice, and tolerance.

Would such a radical plan discourage work? Would it encourage goofing off, gambling, drugs, and drink?

Possibly. We have plenty of that now in the present "system." If you did offer something like stimmig and made the grant universal, not taxable, *and* you did not reduce it if the person made additional money from a paying job, my bet is that it would work well. The basic grant would be enough to buy food and shelter and pay for health care, education, and retirement, though not enough to live with much luxury. Most, like most middle-class and rich people today, would want to work to make more money. Possibly just to escape boredom—but also to achieve and to "pursue happiness" at a higher income level. And they would be the ones (as they are now) who pay the taxes on incomes greater than their base grant and thus finance the whole scheme. Everyone now would be free "to salt down their [own] fish as calmly as a Gloucester man salts down his fish."

Even the environment might benefit, because many more people would welcome the opportunity to be like Henry David Thoreau and spend more time "inspecting snowstorms" and "looking after the wildlife of the town."

Facts Are Better than Dreams

● ● ●

Mar 28, 2016

Winston Churchill wrote, "Facts are better than dreams."
Henry David Thoreau was also a good quote maker. He wrote in *Walden,*

> Say what you have to say, not what you ought. Any truth is better than make-believe. Tom Hyde, the tinker, standing on the gallows, was asked if he had anything to say. 'Tell the tailors,' said he, 'to remember to make a knot in their thread before they take the first stitch.' His companion's prayer is forgotten.

Both quotes apply these days to our relations with Islam. The unsaid and unwelcome truth is that Islamic civilization is grossly inferior to our Western civilization today—just as communism/socialism is grossly inferior to market-based capitalism in supporting and advancing our Modern Age. But the Green/Progressive clergy insists on multicultural fiction and politically-correct speech that denies these obvious truths.

As un-PC as it is, I've said it and am glad. Thoreau is right, "Truth is better than make believe."

Last year I wrote,

> Religious people say that, above all, they trust God's words in the Bible. Usually they are selective though. They trust the passages

that promise love and eternal life but ignore the ones that praise slavery, recommend sinners be stoned to death, or claim God destroyed an entire city because of its *wickedness*. (Muslims too are selective too, but many today *do* pay attention to the nastier passages in their versions of Allah's words in their Quran.)

Jane and I have visited in Muslim countries like Morocco, Mali, and Turkey. Most of the Muslims we met there were like most Christians we met in Europe—moderate, decent, and peaceful. Some Muslims we met took their religion more seriously and prayed often in mosques. They are like Christians who often pray in church but don't follow the dogmas that closely in their daily lives. Both sum up their religion as loving your neighbors, doing good, and praying for peace, prosperity, and personal goals.

With the terrorist attacks increasing recently, Obama, Clinton, Sanders, and most Democrats are right in cautioning us not to panic and lose faith in our own strengths. Terrorism is a strategy of weakness and losers. But, alas, it sometimes works.

But we do have to face facts. We are in a religious war now. Pussyfooting around and not calling it by its right name is not helpful either. Radical Islamists hate our guts and want to kill us. Despite the evidence from our travels, even moderate Muslims are a little like *true believers* and don't look that kindly on Christians or members of any other religion. They resemble Christians in Germany under the Nazis who may not have known or approved of the Holocaust but who thought Jews, gypsies, and gays were bad people. Moderate Muslims may not approve of murder and terrorism, but they do think Christians, Jews, Hindus, atheists, or members of any religion except Islam are not only misled but are bad people. (I realize that is a bit of an exaggeration when it comes to many American Muslims, especially African American ones, many of whom have died defending the USA either in the police or the armed forces in war. I apologize to these patriots.)

In addition while Muslims do consider Jesus a true prophet and believe in the Bible, the Quran is really not much like the New Testament.

Unlike Jesus, Mohammed was a fierce warrior who advised his followers to be fierce warriors. One result is that today's Muslims are better known for violence and war than for peace and freedom.

It was not always so. In medieval days in the Middle East, Africa, and especially in Asia, Muslim countries were in many ways had a superior culture. They were more tolerant, had better health care, more advanced science, and were more creative in the arts. Today, the opposite is true. Islam has never had a real Renaissance, Reformation, or Enlightenment. Islamic countries are sometimes rich in oil and gas but are grossly inferior in culture.

They keep the female half of their population in permanent submission. Women have to wear special clothing to cover their bodies and heads, are not permitted to drive cars, or shop in the marketplaces, have to accept arranged marriages, and permanent submission to the husband(s) (men are often encouraged to have more than one submissive wife). Islamic countries have few or no civil liberties or rights for minority faiths. Islamic countries today are woefully lacking in creative achievement in science, technology, literature, or any of the arts (when Muslims emigrate to the West many do achieve and at a very high level indeed!) Many Muslims want to impose repressive sharia laws wherever they live. All this is unfortunately true for both radical and moderate Muslims. The small minority of really radical Muslims wants to terrorize and kill us.

Unfortunately Muslims also have much higher birth rates than Christians or the unchurched. They also start reproducing much earlier. In time this demographic fact will inevitably transform most Western European countries into Islamic majorities with all that implies for the Modern Age lifestyles and political government.

We in the West still have a strong commitment to freedom of and from religion. We preach respect for all faiths, even atheism. Islam does the opposite. It reminds me of similar conflicts in the Cold War competition between democracy and communism and socialism that never have been totally resolved in Europe or America.

The stickiest problem is really how to deal with *true believers* of any faith, whether they believe in little green men on the moon, the Quran, the Bible, Karl Marx, or the modern Progressive-Green clergy. We do have to honor our commitment to freedom and tolerance *even* to people who want to destroy that freedom and tolerance.

I humbly suggest though we don't need to kowtow to true believers of any stripe. We also don't have to follow their example and persecute them. There is a fine line between respect and approval. I can respect people's faith and sincerity in religion, secular or theistic. But I don't need to approve of them in politically correct speech thought, or action.

Both Islam and Christianity have billions of adherents around the world. Socialism also has billions of sympathizers around the world. Green-Progressives have millions of approving voters in the West. Do all of these facts make them right? Hardly! Does that make me right in opposing them? No! Let's discuss it. I think I do have more facts on my side and I do not approve of any *true beliefs*.

"Facts are better than dreams."

Time-Space Prisons

● ● ●

April 13, 2015

MANY YEARS AGO I HAD a political argument with a young, well-traveled liberal friend. In frustration (I think she was losing a Cold War argument) she claimed, "Bill, you don't know what you are talking about. You've never even traveled outside the United States." In other words, I was a prisoner of space.

More recently, a bright biracial college-student friend and in-law hated my blog on racism. She wrote, "I'm insulted that you are pretending to know a single thing about black people." She further advised me to shun Fox News and have more "radical empathy" with the "single mother on the South Side of Chicago." In other words, I was a prisoner of space and time.

Both criticisms make me aware how much we are all in prisons of time and space (this includes Fox News, CNN, PBS, NBC, CBS, ABC, and all other news outlets). Well-traveled people like Jane and I have a slight advantage in space, and old codgers like Jane and I have a slight advantage in time. But all of us, like Plato's cave dwellers, are really stuck in the here and now and barely able to squint and see the world as it is. Read and travel more widely, and we may be able to see a tiny bit more clearly in our space-time prisons.

I read, for instance, that in the ten-thousand-year-long Agricultural Age, a few aristocrats, warriors, and merchants did travel many miles on horseback to make war or trade goods, usually luxury ones for rich lords, ladies, and clergy. I also read that most people over that immense time span were yoked to the earth as serfs, peasants, or slaves and rarely traveled more than a few miles from where they were born. The well-travelled merchants and warriors were the leaders of change and progress.

A few scientists, like Jared Diamond, argue that the West's European Judeo-Christian civilization is not based on any cultural and racial superiority. We in the presently rich West were just lucky to have a more hospitable natural environment for our ancestors' growth and progress than did native people in Africa, Asia, the Americas, or the South Pacific.

I'm not sure about the racial or cultural superiority, but I don't believe it was all environments either. Africa, Asia, and the Americas had and still do have more natural resources (maybe at least as many smart people too) than Europe does. Far more diversity in natural resources too. Countries on these continents are now catching up to the West by adopting Western ideas and policies. I argue instead that it was not geography or natural resources or a more hospitable natural environment, but three specific advantages we in the West had: (1) freedom of and from religion (coming from our history in the Reformation and Enlightenment), (2) encouragement of science and technology (coming out of our unique history in the Renaissance with scientists (natural philosophers) like Copernicus, Galileo, and Newton), and (3) free-market economics (coming out of our history in Christian medieval monasteries and Adam Smith's and other Enlightenment philosopher's genius in the Enlightenment). When these three got into synergy, as they did a little over two hundred years ago in North America, the free world blossomed, and we entered the Modern Age. We in the United States, uniquely founded by these very ideas, led the way. That's why we can justifiably call this country exceptional.

The only places today not following our exceptional leadership are Muslim countries in the Middle East, Asia, and Africa, along with a few Green-Progressive and Marxist socialist/communist leaders in the West. The Muslim countries today are handicapped by an exclusive monotheistic faith that never had a Reformation or Enlightenment as Christianity did.

Radical Muslims and radical Greens-Progressives seem to be stuck today in reactionary fantasies—Agricultural Age idea ditches—while most in the West (and many in non-Western countries like Japan, China, India, Singapore, and South Korea) have followed the United States example and have moved on to the springtime warmth of the Modern Age.

Just in my lifetime I have seen immense changes. Talented blacks, talented women, and other minorities in this country have made enormous progress. Very recently, talented LGBT individuals are also beginning to make great strides.

As to the more distant past, my reading tells me that *every* country in the world, Western or not, had racism, sexism, slavery, and homophobia in spades for thousand of years past. Our Western civilization still has remnants (memes) of all these faults. But less—far less—of all these destructive and reactionary memes which are fast on their way to oblivion.

In the middle of the nineteenth century, we were the first country with large numbers of enslaved people to liberate them. Latin America, the Caribbean Islands, and Asia all imported far more Africans to enslave than North America did, and most took longer to free them. Some countries like England and France did free their slaves and banned the slave trade earlier than the United States did—but they had many fewer slaves in the first place. After liberation, it is true that our Southern states had Jim Crow laws and lynching to keep black people down, but that, too, effectively ended with effective Civil Rights laws of the 1960s. Slavery and its close cousins, serfdom, peasantry, and extreme poverty, still survive in many Muslim countries in Africa and Asia, only now struggling to move out of the Agricultural Age.

Violence, too, has decreased in my lifetime. Today we rightly mourn the deaths of hundreds or even thousands in Iraq or Afghanistan. In my youth we lost more than fifty thousand marines in a battle for the one small island of Iwo Jima. We in the West also lost millions defeating Hitler and Hirohito. And never forget the fact that fascist and communist dictators killed many millions more in their own countries in holocausts, slave labor camps, massacres, and government-induced famines.

Even these crimes are puny compared to percentage casualties in the near-constant Agricultural Age wars. I read that in the Thirty Years' War between Catholics and Protestants in the early seventeenth century, *over a third* of the population in northern Europe perished. In the many ancient Greek, Egyptian, Roman, Mongol, iking, and Persian wars it was common practice to massacre *all* the inhabitants of conquered cities, including children. It was also common practice to grant all warriors free access to rape all women in conquered villages, towns and cities.

We are rightly appalled by the many beheadings, kidnappings, tortures, and murders carried out by radical Muslims today. In seventeenth-century England and Europe, Christians also beheaded, tortured, and burned alive hundreds of traitors, witches, and heretics. (Anthropologists tell us that in the Hunting/Gathering Age, tribes not only routinely tortured and massacred enemies—often they ate them as well. Primitive tribes in Africa, South America, and the South Pacific still have to live with torture, massacre, and cannibalism. (Unfortunately this was also true of some Native American tribes before the Europeans came to this continent.)

That brings up still another perplexing question in our space/time quest—given the mistakes and atrocities of past Ages, does the Modern Age need big government to control things? Is a smaller government as proposed by some libertarians even possible, much less desirable?

Calvin Coolidge was president when I was born in 1926. Compared to now, the federal government was tiny, but the economy was growing faster. I have a picture in my study of the summer White House showing Cal and his *two* secretaries sorting mail in a small room over a tiny post office in Vermont.

I read that in the chaotic Civil War days, Lincoln found time to meet with any ordinary citizen who showed up at the White House. Literally anyone could plead his case with the president himself, and hundreds did.

All this evidence from my reading suggests that the present bloated size of the government now is due not to modernity or the Modern Age, but comes more directly out of Roosevelt's New Deal ideas and policies of the 1930s.

In 2016, the United States is still the leader of the free world in freedom, science, technology, and free-market economics—what I call the Modern Age. It is unseemly to boast, but it's dangerous to be falsely modest or to rest on our laurels. As Lincoln claimed in the midst of the darkest days of the Civil War, we are still "the last best hope of earth."

Paving Stones on the Slippery Slope

• • •

Aug. 3, 2015

I WENT TO A VERY left-liberal college—Antioch. I liked my time there very much. Most of my professors and friends were lefties, some were socialists, and a few were communists. So, too, the majority of my friends and colleagues during the course of eighteen years of teaching were left-leaning Democrats. I was, too.

With only a few exceptions, I found my leftist professors, students, teachers, and friends to be thoughtful, intelligent, and kind people. Invariably they had good intentions. One of the saddest and most poignant tragedies of the twentieth century, though, is the way leftist dogma that had such good intentions has so often paved a slippery slope to hell.

Most leftists (liberals, socialists, and communists), for instance, are very hard on fascism's atrocities but find it alarmingly easy to ignore some of the arguably worse nightmares in recent human history brought on by socialist left-leaning governments: the slave labor camps, massacres, and government-induced famines of Lenin's and Stalin's Soviet Union; the brutality, massacres and government-induced famines of Mao's China; Kim Jong-un's absurd antics and famines in North Korea; Pol Pot's genocides in Cambodia; Fidel Castro's bungling atrocities in Cuba; and Hugo Chavez's copycat revolution in Venezuela that has devastated a fine country. In some cases leftists have even been lavish in their praise. Lincoln Steffens, a famous left-leaning journalist, wrote from a luxurious Swiss spa after a short trip to the new Soviet Union of Lenin's work, "I have seen the future, and it works."

I summarize here current dogmas of the leftist faith (note: I still believe *some* of them).

Keep an open mind and defend liberty and equality. Government can and should help in that quest. Classic liberalism—freedom, that is—makes the Modern Age distinctly modern. I agree.

Make sure the open mind is usually a politically correct, left-liberal Democratic one. One liberal friend expressed this as, "I don't see why any thinking person would ever vote Republican." Not a good rule.

Accept individuals without prejudice for their race, color, sex, sexual preference, religion, ethnicity, or nationality. Martin Luther King Jr. wanted his children "not be judged by the color of their skin, but by the content of their character." I agree. I think this is a good rule that should be followed by all citizens of any democracy.

Lenin, Stalin, Mao, and Castro went too far, but they had good intentions and were Progressives who were on the people's side. Reagan, Thatcher, Chang Kai-shek, and Nixon were corrupt reactionaries who were on the side of the rich. Statements like this are wildly exaggerated or simply false.

Recent prosperity in China and India is due to their abundant talent and resources. This is certainly not true. Talents and resources were wasted under socialism, but free markets used them to create wealth and prosperity after decades of tyranny, misery, and famine under Marxist-style socialism.

CEOs are overpaid and live in slothful luxury. NFL quarterbacks, NBA stars, and rap singers make a lot of money, but they earn it and have cool lifestyles. Not accurate.

Not obligatory but recommended for left-liberals: basketball, fishing, bicycling, rock climbing, smartphones, Facebook, Twitter, Planned Parenthood, the Democratic Party, socialism, abortion, gay marriage, co-ops, immigrants, minimum wages, government and private unions, tattoos, tongue and genital jewelry, sustainability, organic food, farmers' markets, multiculturalism, diversity, marijuana, cocaine, hybrid cars, electric cars, endangered species, Fiji water, the "Hamilton" musical, Bernie Sanders, hip-hop, rap, graffiti, doom-and-gloom scientists, George Soros, nonprofit enterprises.

Not obligatory but *not* recommended for left-liberals: football, baseball, hunting, horse racing, golf, print media, plastics, casinos, luxury cars, corporations, television, rich people, the Republican Party, the Tea Party, babies, entrepreneurs, CEOs, prisons, fossil fuels, big banks, police, guns, the military, bottled water, natural climate change, GM foods, Donald Trump, shopping malls, junk mail, optimistic scientists, small businesses, Wall Street, the Heritage Foundation, the Koch brothers, the "My Fair Lady" musical; oil and gas companies, Fox News, Exxon-Mobil, profit-making corporations in general.

Calling attention to "racial gaps" in schools and prison statistics is Progressive, but calling attention to "racial gaps" in the NBA and Olympic track teams is racist. Calling attention to college affirmative-action programs is okay, but calling attention to quotas for Jews, Asians, and whites is racist. Any reference to bell curves or IQs is racist.

Genes may be important, but education and environment are more important. Education and environment are the long-term answers to most problems. (Not coincidentally, they also provide comfortable living to the modern clergy—teachers, professors, administrators, government bureaucrats, politicians, scientists and non-profit administrators.)

Jewish and Asian superiority in academia, science, media, business, and the arts should be downplayed, and calling attention to any lack of achievement in these same areas for minority groups is a strict no-no.

Solar and wind energy are good; fossil fuels, nuclear energy, and hydroelectric dams are bad.

Ecology and environmental sciences are reliable and good; engineering, physics, biology, genetics, and chemistry are at best suspect and at worst, dangerous and bad.

Recycling, rejecting plastic bags, carbon-footprint advice, and population controls are good. Travel by plane or auto, second homes, and luxury-living are bad—unless the high livers make up for their sins by buying carbon offsets.

Organic and natural are good; chemical and artificial are bad.

Bell curves are OK when applied to the nonliving or to plants and animals; when applied to humans, they are racist, sexist, and homophobic.

Spirituality is fine; religion is suspect. Mocking Christian beliefs is okay; mocking Muslim beliefs is not okay.

Zoos are bad; wilderness parks are good.

The Sierra Club, the Audubon Society, the Wilderness Society, the Democratic Party, MoveOn.org, and most environmental and Progressive groups are unbiased and trustworthy. The Heritage Foundation, the Cato Institute, the Heartland Institute, the Koch brothers, and any groups supported by oil companies or conservative rich donors are biased and should not be taken seriously.

The Koch brothers are trying to buy elections; George Soros is supporting democracy.

The *New York Times*, PBS, the *New Yorker* magazine, the *Huffington Post*, and the BBC are credible, professional, and unbiased. Fox News, the *Wall Street Journal* editorial page, the Drudge Report, and talk radio are biased and not credible. Jon Stewart, Bill Maher, Rachel Maddow, Dr. Dre, Beyoncé, and Eminem are intelligent and charming; Rush Limbaugh, Bill O'Reilly, Charles Koch, Sarah Palin, and Donald Trump are stupid and disgusting.

Absurd Theatre

● ● ●

June 27, 2016

FOR MANY YEARS I HAVE been a devotee of Absurd theatre. I directed a high school production of *Waiting for Godot*, the justly famous play of the Irish writer Samuel Beckett. I acted (a bit part) in a professional Milwaukee Rep production of *The Killer* by the Romanian playwright Eugene Ionesco. I also directed Ionesco's play *Rhinoceros* with high school actors. A professional summer theatre that I founded produced a number of absurd plays including N. F. Simpson's *A Resounding Tinkle*, Edward Albee's *Zoo Story*, and the Swiss playwright Max Fritsch's *Herr Biedermann and the Firebugs* Another of Ionesco's contributions that I am fond of is the one-act play, *The Chairs*. I have seen, laughed, and cried with it many times.

I go into this in some detail here to demonstrate I know what I'm talking about when it comes to absurd theatre.

When it comes to the absurd in every day modern life you only need to look around you or read the newspapers! A few glaring examples:

The absurdly unlikely alliance between Greens and Progressives today that almost everyone in the media avoids mentioning. Progressives like Hilary Clinton, Bernie Sanders, and President Obama say they want to see the economy grow, create more jobs, enlarge the middle class, redistribute wealth, and reduce poverty. They *say* that climate change is the most important challenge of our time. I don't really believe them. Because,,,

The Democratic Greens motto is, "a growing economy means a shrinking ecosystem." I do believe the Greens when they say they want above all else to: *shrink* the economy, *reduce* the population, *use fewer* resources, *leave all* fossil fuels in the ground, and as Pope Francis advises, "significantly limit consumption" to save the poor and the living earth.

If that's not a recipe for an absurd political pairing I don't know what is!

And then there is to yawing gap between ideas and actual behavior in people enamored of Green dogma. The most dedicated middle or upper class Green would not consider getting rid of their ski lodge, their cabin in the woods, or their second home in Florida or Arizona—much less give up flying or driving to them or other equally glamorous spots for business, family or pleasure. They are also the first to object to any cuts in their salaries or benefits. Summing up, they, like most people in the world, have little desire to "significantly limit consumption." The Greens do imagine that an all-powerful government (controlled by Democrats of course) can do it all somehow someway with no need to change their personal lifestyle or lower their *carbon footprints.*

If that's not a recipe for absurdity, I don't know what is!

Not to mention the Progressives reluctance to identify our mortal enemy as Radical Islam. Progressives take delight in mocking Trump's modest proposal to limit potential Muslim immigration, calling it racist and intolerant of religious differences and not worthy of a free society. Not recognizing that today's Radical Islamists and even many Moderate Muslims breed sexism, racism and intolerance the world over.

And then there is the meek acceptance by major corporate CEO's and conservative politicians of *sustainability* in their thinking and their advertising when it is plainly designed to put their companies out of business.

Or take the educational world where professors lobby to enroll more students and make their colleges more *sustainable* (and expensive). At the same time they want the administration (or the government) to increase the salaries and decrease their workloads.

And there is the contrast between editorial content and advertising content in liberal newspapers and magazines. The advertising is directed at the top tenth of one percent of the wealthy and their trophy wives; the editorial content is a leftist rant against inequality. It's one more example of the left's infatuation with socialism and equality of outcome despite its history of misery and abject failures in China, India, South America and Soviet bloc countries.

Finally I marvel at the gap between the left-liberal clergy's good intentions and the reality of inner city violence, racism and squalor. The Progressive-Green clergy has been in power nationally and locally in our major cities for decades, and they keep repeating the same tired promises. When confronted with the reality of inner city violence, racism and squalor (and ever-rising prison populations) they simply point to their good intentions and are silent about remedies. To top it off the majority of the minority poor believe them.

If all these are not recipes for absurdity I don't know what is!

To top off this depressing list of modern day absurdities I honestly think I have shown possible ways to advance the Modern Age. I admit now that this may well be the most absurd belief of all.

In Ionesco's one-act play *The Chairs* an Old man and Old woman (the last two people on earth?) are preparing a seaside hall, arranging the chairs for a visit of a distinguished "orator" who is going to reveal the "meaning of life" to "everyone." No one actually comes to sit on the chairs. Just before the "orator" appears the Old man and Old woman, happy at last that their all-important message is about to be revealed—commit suicide by jumping out the windows into the ocean.

The anti-climax comes when the orator does arrive on stage. He turns out to be a deaf-mute and can only mutter meaningless grunts.

I flatter myself that I am like the orator; I do have an important message for the country and the world. Alas, I am deaf and can even recognize signs of muteness!

I can still handle ideas though and I can still write important messages (with the aid of my computer). With my blogs I even have the supremely arrogant idea that I have solved some of the *meanings of life* with my insights into the evolution of human societies and the transitions that have led us to the Modern Age.

But again, like Ionesco's Orator—I remain a deaf-mute trying to speak to an invisible audience!

Science and "Soylent Green"

● ● ●

July 20, 2015

Jane and I watched a DVD last week called *Soylent Green*. If not the worst movie we have seen, it surely ranks in the bottom ten. It was released in 1973, five years after Paul Ehrlich's best-selling book was published, *The Population Bomb*. Ehrlich predicted that hundreds of millions would starve to death in the 1970s; that sixty-five million of them would be Americans; that India and China were doomed to famines; and that odds were good that England would probably not exist in the year 2000.

Based on a science-fiction novel of 1966, *Soylent Green* purports to show what New York City would be like just seven years from now in 2022. There will be, the movie predicts, forty million people in the city; you won't be able to go down a stairway without stumbling on a homeless wretch; the few rich will have hot water, air conditioning (and beautiful women as built-in furniture) in their luxury suites; the vast majority poor will suffer in the streets with heat, violence, pollution, and deep poverty; the only food for the masses will be wafers of Soylent green (advertised as made from ocean plankton but actually made from corpses of people scooped up by giant garbage "scoopers" in periodic raids ordered by rich, corporate-supported fascist dictators).

It's a nightmare, all right. But the message is similar to the one the Green Sustainable religion, including Pope Francis, is spreading now. We have to stop (or even better, reverse) growth. This means in practice to live simpler lives, "significantly limiting our consumption," as the pope says. In addition, we need to recycle scarce resources; go organic in our agriculture and natural in our manufacturing; control and reduce population; rein in science and technology; step up regulations on industry and commerce; and, in the most recent addition, cut back and eventually abandon fossil fuels. If we don't act soon on all of these, say the proponents, we are surely heading for a nightmare as depicted in *Soylent Green*.

I think the opposite is more likely. If we *follow* the advice of the Green-Progressive religion I think we may well end up in a world like *Soylent Green*. Exacerbated by the growing and greater Muslim population, the world everywhere will be similar to the world everywhere in the Agricultural Age. The lords and ladies of government, supported by the modern clergy, will be in charge, and most of us will be serfs, slaves, or peasants, with all that implies.

President Obama's chief science adviser is physicist John Holdren. He is one of the leaders of the new Green-Progressive religion. He joined with biologist Paul Ehrlich on the first Earth Day to warn us that I = PAT, population times affluence times technology equals environmental impact, (and ruin).

In the sixties and seventies, the doomsday emphasis was on overpopulation and resource scarcity. Many of us oldsters remember the gas lines under Jimmy Carter, lines that mysteriously disappeared under Ronald Reagan. Today gasoline is more plentiful, and the doomsayers have a different bogeyman—climate change.

I hesitate to speculate on what motivates these distinguished scientists and filmmakers to predict nightmares like this. I suspect it is simple self-interest. Like most of the left-liberal Green-Progressive clergy, they stand to benefit from modern *government* growth just as the clergy in medieval times benefited from feudal power and wealth. I also realize that bad news and violence are more popular (and profitable) than good news. Whatever the motives, their evidence is weak, and their recommendations are directly and devastatingly destructive.

Take their evidence first:

Populations in wealthy countries have not exploded. If anything, were it not for migrations, populations in developed are imploding. Population growth in poor countries has lessened, and the richer countries become, the more it levels off. Besides that, there is little evidence that population size or growth has anything to do with economic or environmental health. If anything, the rich countries with the densest and largest populations and the most technology are the most peaceful and creative—and the least polluted. The converse is also true: the most polluted, violent and uncreative are the poor countries with the lowest density, the strongest religion, and the least technology.

Resource scarcity was a big issue in the twentieth century. Today, energy, food, and natural resources are more plentiful than ever, and there are fewer people living in abject poverty. When I was born in 1926, one out of four people on Earth lived on less than a dollar a day. Today, even taking inflation into account, only one out of twenty lives on the equivalent of less than a dollar a day, even though the world population has more than tripled. Both China and India are self-sufficient in food now despite the dire predictions of Ehrlich and others. Once they abandoned the phony religious appeal of socialism and sustainability and adopted free-market capitalist ways, both China and India are fast growing into economic superpowers.

Where does all that new wealth come from? The answer of course is that wealth comes primarily from human hands and minds and not from any other natural resource.

I know many scientists claim the evidence for climate change is overwhelming, just as many in the twentieth century claimed the same for overpopulation and resource scarcity. But despite the melting glaciers, the average temperature on Earth has not changed for eighteen years. Extreme weather (tornadoes, hurricanes, etc.) has become *less* frequent, not more. And whatever happens over the next century, climates on Earth have been changing for millennia, and spending huge amounts of time, talent, and money today trying to prevent change a hundred years from now is a classic fool's errand.

Recommendations of Green activists remind me of the proverb "No good deed goes unpunished." Or better yet, "The road to hell is paved with good intentions."

Taken literally (fortunately, few followers do) the Green recommendations are more likely to bring wars, poverty, disease, violence, and environmental disasters—in othere words a return to the Agriculture Age and more *Soylent Greens*. To further the Modern Age, we need instead to support science and technology, reduce regulations on industry and commerce, and not worry so much about population or resources (except for fostering the ultimate resource, human creativity which is the ultimate source of all new wealth). Climate change or not, we can safely use fossil fuels for years or even centuries to come.

If you want to see my projections, not for a few decades, but for a few centuries, see the first three blogs in this book. I confidently predict that when the Modern Age has passed over its growing pains, and that the three truly Progressive factors—science and technology, free-market capitalism, and freedom of religion paired with freedom from religion—will have demonstrated their full potential and the future will be sunny and cool and not at all like *Soylent Green*.

Middle Class Blues

● ● ●

Dec. 9, 2013

"Every family would be middle class." That was my message if we adopted a stimmig plan. Some think that would be utopia. Others aren't so sure.

In terms of income, the majority in this country is middle class. That is, they have incomes of less than three hundred thousand dollars but more than thirty thousand dollars a year. (In my youth in the fifties, the second figure was closer to three thousand dollars a year, which tells you how much economic growth and inflation there has been the last sixty-plus years.)

If you define it in terms of values, it's different. Many artists, musicians, writers, actors, and intellectuals (like me) have incomes closer to the poverty range but don't think of themselves as poor. Many are noted for mocking middle-class hypocrisy and values. When Harold Ross launched the *New Yorker* magazine, he wrote that the new magazine was not going to be edited for "little old ladies in tennis shoes in Dubuque." Check the arts section of the *New York Times* (or the *New York Times Magazine* or *Book Review*) this week for many more examples of middle-class mockery.

When it comes to politics, it gets murkier. Both parties claim to be for the middle classes because that is where the votes are. Jonathan Haidt, a social psychologist from New York University, says the Tea Party is basically a middle-class movement.

He claimed that the Tea Party is made of "libertarians" (who prize freedom above all) and conservatives (who prize *karma* as their guiding principle). He wrote,

> The notion of karma," he explains, "comes with lots of new-age baggage, but it is an old and very conservative idea. It is the Sanskrit word for 'deed' or 'action.' And the law of karma says that for every action, there is an equal and morally commensurate reaction. Kindness, honesty and hard work will (eventually) bring good fortune; cruelty, deceit and laziness will (eventually) bring suffering. No divine intervention is required; it's just a law of the universe, like gravity. [12]

My mom and dad probably would have agreed.

Compared to that of my youth in the forties and fifties, American culture as a whole *has* become more tolerant, less violent, better educated, more middle class, and richer today with less pollution. We have also become more vulgar, more dependent on the government, and more lower class in lifestyle. Long hair for men came in with the Beatles in the early sixties, but today many in the middle and upper classes escalate the trend with tattoos, rings in their noses and lips, and sloppy prison-type clothes—not to mention single parentage, sexual freedom, college educations, and frequent use of the four-letter words (all of which were rare in my youth).

Many today, in a rush of multicultural tolerance, seem to be admiring and sometimes imitating what our ancestors called savages (the politically incorrect description of primitive hunting-gathering tribes). See the popularity of movies like *The Hunger Games* and *Avatar.*

The contrast between elite- and lower-class lifestyles is shown comically in George Bernard Shaw's play *Pygmalion* (the source of the *My Fair Lady* musical). Henry Higgins, the upper-class professor, on a bet is trying to make Eliza Doolittle, a poor flower girl, into a lady by teaching her

---

12 Haidt, Jonathan, *The Righteous Mind* (2013).

to speak properly. Eliza's father, the dustman Alfred Doolittle, doesn't think much of the project:

> I'm one of the undeserving poor: that's what I am. Think of what that means to a man. It means that he's up against middle class morality all the time. If there's anything going, and I put in for a bit of it, it's always the same story: 'You're undeserving; so you can't have it.' But my needs is as great as the most deserving widow's that ever got money out of six different charities in one week for the death of the same husband. I don't need less than a deserving man: I need more. I don't eat less hearty than him and I drink a whole lot more. What is middle class morality? Just an excuse for never giving me anything...I ain't pretending to be deserving. I'm undeserving; and I mean to go on being undeserving.

When Alfred comes into an inheritance from an eccentric American millionaire that catapults him into the middle class (as stimmig might do). He is pissed.

> Who asked him to make a gentleman of me? I was happy. I was free. I touched pretty nigh everybody for money when I wanted it, same as I touched you, Henry Higgins...A year ago I hadn't a relative in the world except two or three that wouldn't speak to me. Now I've fifty, and not a decent week's wages among the lot of them. I have to live for others and not for myself: that's middle class morality.

Higgins's mother suggests he just turn the money down (or with stimmig, you don't have to take the checks).

> That's the tragedy of it, ma'am. It's easy to say chuck it; but I haven't the nerve. Which of us has? We're all intimidated. Intimidated, ma'am: that's what we are...If I was one of the deserving poor,

and had put by a bit, I could chuck it...But I, as one of the undeserving poor, have nothing between me and the pauper's uniform but this here blasted three thousand a year that shoves me into the middle class...They've got you every way you turn: it's a choice between the Skilly of the workhouse and the Char Bydis of the middle class; and I haven't the nerve for the workhouse. Intimidated: that's what I am.

How would stimmig be for you?

Ideas and the Economy

• • •

Nov. 30, 2015

EVOLUTION IN SOCIETIES, DIVIDING THE vast and mysterious world of human history into three major ages, is a giant step forward. The simplification helps make sense of climate change, racism, terrorism, and basic economics. For a summary of the three ages, I suggest you reread the blogs in the first sections of this book.

Here are my final thoughts on basic economics.

I start by apologizing to the left-liberal clergy, whom I often skewer in these blogs. They are on the side of the angels when it comes to many issues today. They (and I) are for a secular government, for tolerance and compassion, for democracy, freedom of and from religion, environmental health, civil liberties and rights, notwithstanding some recent college flaps when extremists enforced PC speech by excluding those who disagreed. They are also opposed to religious tyranny, racism, and, even if lukewarmly, they support free markets, free trade, and the profitable exchanges of capitalism. They (and I) have good intentions—always.

How many can say as much?

I'm tempted to answer—billions.

Unfortunately, that's not true. Not even close.

Radical Muslims don't. Even many moderate Muslims don't. And Muslims, moderate or radical, make up at least a quarter of all the human beings who live on this planet! Many in both camps, moderate and radical, believe firmly that Allah should be obeyed by keeping women in head scarves and abject submission to the man; mocking the Prophet Mohammed should be forbidden under pain of death; anyone who commits adultery or fornication should be publicly stoned; and we would be better off with Sharia Law. I know not all Muslims follow these beliefs just as not all Christians follow through on Jesus's advice to live in poverty and chastity. Unlike lukewarm Christians, even moderate Muslims are reluctant to blend into secular societies. Many Muslims are convinced that Christians and Jews are wrong and even evil and that Israel in particular should be wiped off the face of the Earth. Note that Muslim anti-Semitism (which some Christians share) does not come from medieval ancestors. Islam in those days was more tolerant than Christianity was.

By and large, Islam today is not interested in joining the Modern Age—except perhaps to enjoy the technology and the wealth we have created in the West. These judgments are not politically correct but have the advantage of being true.

But alas, the same is true of radical Christians, Socialists, Greens, and communists—in fact, radical *true believers* of *any* persuasion. They want to convince you, or, if they have the power, force you to follow their rules, whether you and they are Christian, Muslim, PC, Green, Progressive, Nazi, Jewish, or whatever true belief.

The wisdom of the division of history into three ages is most obvious when it comes to the economy. In both the Hunting/Gathering and the Agricultural Ages, wealth was like a big pie—if one gets a bigger piece (the strong and the rich), all others will have to make do with smaller pieces (be poor). In all early days, wealth was land, gold and slaves. And land, gold and slaves on Earth were all limited. When Europeans first arrived in America, the Native Americans were in transition—many had some agriculture but still relied on hunting and gathering on the always-scarce land for survival. Native Americans were roughly equal within their tribes. But all tribes had to live with violence, poverty, torture, and near-genocidal wars in order to get and hold better land.

In the Agricultural Age, food was more plentiful, but extreme inequality of wealth became the norm. Scarce land, slaves to work the land, and always-scarce gold made for wealth (the big pie). The strongest and most aggressive—lords, ladies, and clergy—were owners and all others (99 percent) worked as merchants, artisans, artists, serfs, slaves, or peasants. As in the earlier Hunting/Gathering Age, violence and wars were everyday realities. In the Agricultural Age, the elite warrior-owners themselves fought to get more land, slaves, and gold. The serfs, slaves, and peasants also stole, fought, and killed often in inevitably futile attempts to get their fair share.

The Modern Age changed all this, but not overnight. Land was no longer necessary for wealth. It is true that Washington, Jefferson, and Madison owned land, gold and slaves when they launched the Modern Age. More important though, they owned memes—new ideas for change that they got from Enlightenment thinkers in Europe like Adam Smith, David Hume, John Locke, and Baron Montesquieu.

The results today are that Warren Buffett, Bill Gates, George Soros, Donald Trump, or the Koch brothers do not base their wealth on land, slaves, or gold. Instead it comes from smart work, science, and technology along with freedom and a bit of luck. They got rich—and the whole world got richer (in capitalism, wealth *does* trickle down). Just as Adam Smith predicted they would get rich by using as he foresaw free markets, diversity of talents, and free trade—in a word, capitalism.

The end result is that now the total wealth of the country or the world is not like a static pie. The pie continually gets bigger, and the wealth trickles down. In fact, the whole world is far richer per capita, even with far more people, than anyone could have dreamed a decade, a hundred, or a thousand years ago.

Some leftists today want to reverse this formula and, in effect if not in intention, return to earlier ages where wealth was like a big pie. (They hope and expect to leave out the bad memes.) Led by Karl Marx (and today by Bernie Sanders and Hillary Clinton and Green *clergy* scientists like John Holdren, James Hansen, Paul Ehrlich, and the late Rachel Carson), this secular Green-Progressive clergy thinks that smart and right-thinking governments can create modern utopias that will share the big pie of wealth. They call it socialism.

A prime example of the superiority of capitalism over socialism is seen in the recent attempt by Pfizer to save on taxes by having a smaller company in Ireland buy a larger American company. Pfizer plans to move their headquarters to Ireland, where corporate taxes are much less than in the United States. The Pfizer CEO says it will be a win-win deal for all. True, the treasury will get a few million less in tax payments, but that money will be more profitably invested by a private company, Pfizer, than by any government. This way the nation and the world will gain jobs and prosperity.

If you, on the other hand, do think the government can better invest that tax money, maybe you should consider a trip to Cuba or Venezuela or North Korea or any Muslim monarchy stuck in the Agricultural Age despite their oil wealth. Follow it up with trips to booming capitalist countries that are progressing today like Japan, South Korea, China, Taiwan, India, Mexico, or Singapore.

Last Intermission

● ● ●

Have you wondered why this book does not have any divisions into sections—like education, politics, economics, environment, history, arts, and sciences? Or perhaps current issues—like climate change, welfare, energy, population, and pollution?

Do you have a special book where you actually write down the user IDs and passwords you need on the Internet? My computer savvy daughter-in-law insisted I needed one, so I tried. But, gosh, it got complicated and eventually totally out of hand. I tried my best to have dividers that would be useful. Like personal, bank, credit card, business, shopping, and the like. So where do you put the user ID and password needed to enter Ameritrade (where I have a small investment account) or Ancestry.com (to which I subscribe) or Constant Contact (which I use to distribute my weekly blog) or the cable company (which supplies my Internet, TV, and telephone)? Yes, I could make separate folders for investments, ancestors, blogs, cable companies, and TV. But then, if you get my drift, when still another user ID and password comes up, say for Green sites or government sites or tax problems, I have the same confusion in spades.

The point is, I did not divide this book into easy sections because the Modern Age does not divide into easy sections. Economics mixes with environmental, which mixes with education, government, politics, history, personal, art, science, psychology, sociology, race, sex, lifestyles, money, life, death, and god knows what else. As the author of *Waiting for Godot* would say—billions!

Blogs don't like pigeonholes. At least *Bill's' Blogs* does not.

"The past is never dead, it's not even past." (a repeat)

• • •

Sept. 16, 2013

Henry Ford said it, "I wouldn't give a nickel for all the history in the world. History is more or less bunk." The philosopher Friedrich Hegel agreed, "The only thing we learn from history is that we learn nothing from history." Even Huck Finn agreed, "by and by she let it out that Moses had been dead a considerable long time: so then I didn't care no more about him, because I don't take no stock in dead people."

I don't agree with Ford, Hegel and Huck Finn. We are living history every day. As William Faulkner put it, "the past is never dead, it's not even past."

Knowing more about past history can't provide detailed road maps to cope with all the knotty problems of the present but it can point us in progressive directions.

We are in the very early stages of a major shift in human life on this small planet—moving from an Agricultural Age that lasted ten thousand years to a Modern Age only a few hundred years in the making. This Modern Age features science and technology, capitalism and free markets, and radical changes in religion and politics.

Here are tastes of what it was like during the Agricultural Age: (the following are quotes from *The History of the Medieval World* by

Susan Wise Bauer. New York: W. W. Norton, 2010.)Heraclius [the Christian king] decided to sue for peace, even if it came on poor terms. He sent envoys to Khosru II [the Persian king], to bring an end to the war. But Khosru II was winning, and he refused. ... He then besieged Jerusalem. The city fell. The Persians, who were irate over the length of the siege, stormed in and massacred the population. ... They destroyed persons of every age, massacred them like animals, cut them in pieces. Families were herded into the dry moat around the city and put under guard until thirst and heat killed them. In all, nearly sixty-seven thousand men, women, and children died under Persian swords.

A few hundred years later Charlemagne (the head of the Holy Roman Empire in Europe) was enforcing his will over western Christian civilization.

> The Saxon resistance to his rule had so angered him that, in 782, he had ordered forty-five hundred Saxon prisoners to be massacred. ... Afterwards Charlemagne decreed that any 'unbaptized Saxon who conceals himself among his people and refuses to seek baptism, but rather choses to remain a pagan shall die.' A Saxon who stole from a church, or did violence to a priest, or indulged himself in the old Saxon rites instead of Christian worship, would be put to death. And any Saxon who did not observe Lent properly would be executed.

The scholar Bernard Bailyn quotes a contemporary on the European colonist's treatment if Native Americans in the 16th century,

> surprisinge them [Native Americans] in their habitations, intercepting them in theire hunting, burning theire townes, demolishing theire temples, destroyinge theire canoes, plucking upp theire wares, carrying away theire corne, and depriving them of whatsoever may yield them succor or relief, by which meanes

in a very short while both your just revenge and your perpetuall security might be certainly effected.

The Natives Americans were equally heartless,

> In plantation after plantation from west to east, north and south of the James, the Indians turned on their unsuspecting hosts, in some places while sharing 'breakfast with people at their tables,' and with axes, hammers, shovels, tools, and knives slaughtered them indiscriminately, 'not sparing eyther age or sexe, man, woman, or childe: so sodaine in their cruell execution that few or none discerned the weapon or blow that brought them to destruction.' ... And the horror was compounded by the attackers 'defacing, dragging, and mangling the dead carcasses into many pieces, and carrying some parts away in derision, with base and brutish triumph.'

Gruesomely fascinating ... but what's the point?

That agricultural age on earth lasted over 10,000 years. We today—just two hundred years into the industrial and scientific age—still carry the genes *and* the memes of our ancestors who lived during this long age. The genes we can't do much about yet.

Many of the memes (that is, the accumulated lessons, languages, habits of mind, ideas, prejudices, loyalties, traditions and quirks) are still with us. In the last two hundred years some have changed, but not everywhere, and not as much as they need to change to advance this Modern Age.

To my mind one of the most important and destructive is still in fashion among powerful groups today—the idea that resources for wealth are severely limited. Any gain to one is a loss to another. It is a zero-sum game. To gain more wealth you have to fight. To solve poverty you take from the rich, and give to the poor.

And in a closely connected meme, since the world is such a terrible and uncertain place the only sure sanctuary is a shared strong religious belief (supernatural or secular).

Today, even in America and Europe, this ancient agriculturally based meme often translates into a modern demagogic class war. Profits are theft. To get more money for the 99% take it from the 1%. Or as the sustainable movement puts it, "We have to learn a green lifestyle. We have to learn that the more we consume the less resources are available for other human beings and other creatures."

The good news is that the big central idea behind this class war—that ancient meme that says wealth and resources are limited—is not true. It used to be true. It was true for over a hundred thousand years in both the Agricultural and Hunting/Gathering days. It is not true today.

What makes it not true today is a combination of three important events in recent world history that have changed the reality, but as yet has only begun to change the minds of modern citizens.

One is the birth of modern science and technology; two is the ascendancy of modern free-market capitalism with its win-win capabilities; three is the evolution of Christianity so that it longer demands exclusive rights to our soul, but allows freedom of religion and freedom from religion.

In light of the above, if I could wave a magic wand and change memes overnight here are my suggestions.

Stop worrying about resources. Wealth used to be based on land, gold and slaves. It's not today. Modern wealth is based on the most important *natural* resource—the human hand and brain (science and technology) freed of religious dogmas and yoked to the win-win profit-making capabilities of modern capitalism. As such resources for wealth today are virtually unlimited.

As corollaries we have: win-win trades are better than theft and war; it's better to help your enemies to compete rather than to rape and pillage them; the win-win transactions of capitalism (profits) work better than the zero-sum ones of socialism (good intentions); in short as President Calvin Coolidge said, "profits and civilization go hand in hand."

Governments are important and democratic ones are better than authoritarian ones primarily because democratic ones are homeostatic—that is, self-correcting. But beware of giving governments too much power and authority over our lives. Even with the best intentions and the most brilliant and compassionate of executives, legislators and judges—governments (even democratic ones) can harm as well as help.

And finally, religion is best when stripped of exclusive claims and dogmatic theology, and focused instead on kindness, forgiveness, justice, compassion and love. (This is true of both supernatural ones and secular ones like communism, socialism and environmentalism.)

History is not the bunk. You don't need to take stock in dead people but when you look closely, Faulkner was right, "the past is never dead, it's not even past."

The Three-Second Rule (a repeat as well)

• • •

Jan. 23, 2012

DESPITE MY AFFECTION FOR THE long view and the heavy thinking, I realize that what happens in the next three seconds is what really matters.

Henry David Thoreau put it this way in *Walden*: "In any weather, at any hour of the day or night, I have been anxious to improve the nick of time, and notch it on my stick too; to stand on the meeting of two eternities, the past and future, which is precisely the present moment; to toe that line."

It takes about three seconds for a smile to brighten your day. Or to say "Hello," or "Thank you," or "You're welcome," or "I love you." The time it takes to hug a friend. The time it takes to take a really deep breath, to listen to a song in your head or a beat of your heart. The time it takes to "improve the nick of time…to tow that line."

For most of my life, I have been a future planner. I have not given much time to dwelling on the past, and I rarely consider the present, either. Now that I am old, I am beginning to realize how important the next three seconds are.

A scientist agrees.

Emese Nagy, a developmental psychologist at the University of Dundee, claims, "What we have is very broad research showing that we experience the world in about these three-second time frames."

The three-second rule came to its greatest prominence in basketball. The rule there says you cannot stay in the free-throw lane under the opponent's basket for more than three seconds. Another version says that for safe driving, you should keep at least three seconds' worth of driving time between you and the car ahead of you. Still another applies to dating. If you see a girl (or a guy) you think you might like to date, you have three seconds to make up your mind to approach her (or him). If you delay more than that, your chances of connecting fall off by powers of ten.

I don't think this means you should never plan, or read, or work, or engage in a conversation that takes more than three seconds. Just pay more attention and punctuate your longer plans with three-second phrases.

In my retirement years, my wife and I get our exercise by walking the dog and going swimming at a nearby indoor pool for seniors. I never was a very good swimmer and still am not. But I enjoy and profit from the three-second rule by swimming laps with a leisurely backstroke. I coordinate my arm and leg movements to deep breaths. Breathe in, reach, kick, breathe out; breathe in, reach, kick, breathe out; breathe in, reach, kick, breathe out. Every deep breath and cool glide takes about three seconds, enough time to sneak in a bit of meditation and idea generation for the next week's blog. It's actually the time of day I feel most healthy.

How often do we really look at one another? Or really listen?

Again—Thoreau wrote, "Could a greater miracle take place than for us to look through each other's eyes for an instant? We should live in all the ages of the world in an hour; ay, in all the worlds of the ages. History, Poetry, Mythology—I know of no reading of another's experience so startling and informing as this would be."

I hinted at this mystery of looking and listening when I quoted Samuel Beckett before the title page of a previous book. As the first act of *Waiting for Godot* ends, a boy comes onstage to bring a message from

Mr. Godot (who never appears in the play). Didi is one of the two homeless tramps that are the main characters in the play.

The boy asks, "What shall I tell Mr. Godot, Sir?"

Didi says, "Tell him you saw us…(*long pause*).... you did see us, didn't you?"

Then there is the story of Michael Gates Gill, who had it all—an Ivy League education, a position as creative director at the world's largest ad agency, a house in the Hamptons, and a six-figure salary. After setbacks and nearing retirement age, he ended up taking a job serving coffee at Starbucks, where his boss was a young African American woman and the daughter of a drug addict. According to him, his unlikely descent in status and money turned out to be the thing that "saved his life." Not sure he calls it that, but one of the things he learned was the importance of living in the three-second zone—serving customers with a smile, relating to fellow employees and bosses with attention and humility, producing goods and services that customers liked, and discovering a new respect for hard work.

An older Black man at out local McDonald's where Jane and I often get milkshakes and French fries, seems to have discovered the same secret as Mr. Gill. He always gives us a friendly smile when he fills the order from as he puts it, "you young folks."

Pleasure often comes in three-second intervals. So does pain. Shakespeare, as always, knew what we are talking about when he wrote in *Much Ado about Nothing*, "There was never yet a philosopher who could endure the toothache patiently."

There is always in life the agony and the ecstasy. The pain of a migraine headache; the delight in a vase of flowers; the chagrin when the *other* team completes a Hail Mary pass in the last second; the pleasure when *your* team completes a Hail Mary pass in the last second; the bitterness of a divorce; the view out the window in the morning after the first snow of the season; the loneliness of a dark, cold night; the shiver when you hear a phrase of music you love; the desperation of unrequited love; the ecstasy of an orgasm.

I think part of my respect for the three-second rule comes from age. In our long-ago nightclub act, Jane and I included a poem by Helen Hoyt called "Rain at Night." Especially now, as we touch in bed, the last lines of that poem haunt me.

One day it will be raining as it rains tonight; the same wind blow—
Raining and blowing on this house wherein we lie: but you and I—
    We shall not hear, we shall not ever know,
      O love, I had forgot that we must die.

Dust and Stars

• • •

Nov. 18, 2013

> It is morning, Senlin says, and in the morning
> When the light drips through the shutters like the dew,
> I arise, I face the sunrise,
> And do the things my fathers learned to do.
> Stars in the purple dusk above the rooftops
> Pale in a saffron mist and seem to die,
> And I myself on a swiftly tilting planet
> Stand before a glass and tie my tie.

TOO BAD THAT CONRAD AIKEN, who wrote the above did not live long enough to learn that maybe there are billions of Earths where light from a nearby sun can "drip through the shutters like the dew."

The *Los Angeles Times* reported last week,

> Using a clever method to detect Earth-size exoplanets they may have missed before, astronomers calculated that 1 in 5 stars like the one at the center of the solar system hosts a planet capable of holding liquid water on its surface and—if it had the right chemical ingredients—supporting life.
>
> The finding, published Monday in the *Proceedings of the National Academy of Sciences*, "represents one great leap toward

the possibility of life, including intelligent life, in the universe," said UC Berkeley astronomer Geoffrey Marcy, who worked on the new study. The results suggest that the Milky Way is home to 11 billion Earth-like planets.

The astronomers are talking about stars in the Milky Way, our galaxy. Because there are billions of other galaxies out there, the chances of "light dripping through the shutters like the dew" on some Earth-like planet somewhere in this cozy, crazy universe increase astronomically!

Of course, even with that huge number of possible Earth-like planets, we can't be that certain any of them will have intelligent life. Scientists tell us that life began on this Earth somewhere in the vicinity of three billion years ago. Animal life did not arrive until about three hundred million years ago, and it has been only a few hundred thousand years ago that modern humans appeared. In other words, intelligent life has been around only a tiny sliver of the time that this spaceship has existed.

Some thinkers wonder about that *intelligent* adjective.

Some ancient Greeks believed in it. In his play *Antigone*, Sophocles has the chorus sing,

> Wonders are many and none is more wonderful than man
> The power that crosses the white sea
> Driven by the stormy wind
> Making a path under surges that threaten to engulf him.

A thousand years, later William Shakespeare put words in the mouth of Macbeth to express a more somber view: "Life's but a walking shadow, a poor player that struts and frets his hour on the stage and then is heard no more. It is a tale told by an idiot, full of sound and fury, signifying nothing."

Pascal, a science giant a century after Shakespeare, also had a darker view: "What a chimera then is man! What a novelty, what a monster, what chaos, what a contradiction, what a prodigy! Judge of all things, feeble earthworm, repository of truth, sewer of uncertainty and error, the glory and the sum of the universe."

And then a favorite author of mine in the modern era, the late doctor-scientist Lewis Thomas, pointed out, "Statistically, the probability of any one of us being here is so small that you'd think the mere fact of existing would keep us all in a contented dazzlement of surprise."

Suppose intelligent life did appear on one those Earth-like planets, and suppose we could communicate with them. What would we say?

Lewis Thomas suggested that if we wanted to put our best foot forward, we should send them some Bach concertos. But if Pascal and Shakespeare were closer to reality, perhaps we maybe should put a more honest foot forward by sending them some pornography or some Hollywood epics with heaps of violence and sex.

And then there is the modern poet I quoted at the beginning, Conrad Aiken. He experienced both extremes. Like Sophocles, Aiken wrote some poetry celebrating intelligence and doing "the things my father learned to do." Yet when Conrad was eleven years old, he heard some shots, went into his parent's room, and discovered that his father, a respected brain surgeon, had shot his mother to death and then killed himself. No one ever had a clue why.

Aiken himself lived a long and successful life, was widely published, and won many awards. Despite his childhood trauma, he never despaired. Before he died in 1973, he designed his own tombstone in the shape of a bench in Savannah, Georgia. It was meant as an invitation to visitors to stop, have a martini, and enjoy the inscriptions, "Give my love to the world" and "Cosmos Mariner—Destination Unknown."

If I were making our introduction to these alien intellectuals, I would send poems of Sophocles, Shakespeare, and Conrad Aiken or maybe the musings of modern scientist-poets like Lewis Thomas, who pointed out that when all is said and done, we humans are made of "dust and the light of a star."

So are they.

Thoughts on Death

● ● ●

Jan. 25, 2016

My wife Jane and I often play a variation on the "gotcha" game. We sing snatches of an old song and try to stump the other to name the song. Usually we fail to stump the other. Last evening I won. Jane didn't know this song.

> Don't give up, Tommy Atkins, be a stout fella,
> Chin up! Cheerio! Carry on!
> Oh, the sun's sure to smile on your tight little isle,
> So hang on to your wits and you'll turn the blitz on Fritz,
> There's a whole world behind you shoutin' stout fella!
> Chin up! Cheerio! Carry on!

It is from the same 1941 musical *Babes on Broadway* that had the more popular hit song, "I like New York in June / How about You?" This "Chin up! Cheerio! Carry On" may not be that great a song, but it does remind me how seriously the democracies were threatened when I was starting high school in 1941. Dictators like Adolf Hitler and Josef Stalin were at their peak of power and influence. France, Poland, Austria, Czechoslovakia, the Balkans, Norway, Belgium, and Holland had all surrendered to the Nazis. The Brits were left to fight alone. They did that magnificently and richly earned the name *stout fellas*.

I, on the other hand, was blissfully naïve and almost totally unaware of the threat. It gives me shivers now when I realize how close our free world came to death rattles.

The moral is that despite my confidence now, there is no guarantee the Modern Age itself will be always benign and democratic.

....

A week ago Jane and I decided it was time to put down our little dog, Frankie. He, like us, is getting old and feeble. Our veterinarian saved him when she flatly refused euthanasia. She said she could not in good conscience put a dog down who had some good years of life left in him.

Jane and I yearn for death at times, too. We learned a lesson with Frankie and will try to hang in there more or less cheerfully for a few more years. I thought and wrote about death long ago. Here are two samples from a poetry book I wrote in my youth, called *a little while aware*.

>there is no time left over
>when a man dies
>that edge we keep honing
>returns to its natural state
>and all the prospects we had in mind
>are gone.

>we are given one song
>in harmony or dissonance
>the song must be ours
>yet not ours alone
>when a tree dies
>the wind no longer sings in the leaves
>but rattles and cracks in the sticks
>no longer a song
>a new tuning of the instrument
>preparing a key
>for who knows what mighty new chorus

....

At least when I die I won't have to endure the chorus of jejune photos and videos (not all are jejune!) posted by friends and acquaintances on Facebook.

I get three newspapers delivered early every morning—the *New York Times*, the *Wall Street Journal*, and the *Wisconsin State Journal*. I used to read them all, but lately I skip lightly through the first two and pay most attention to sports in the third. I should cancel all of them, save money, and get my news as so many do now from the Internet. But being lazy and a procrastinator, I'm not sure I will get around to it. (Companies like the *New York Times* don't make it that easy to *cancel*.)

I did notice the first line of a lead article on a recent front page of the *New York Times*: "The world is awash in crude oil, with enough extra produced last year to fuel all of Britain or Thailand. And the price of oil will not stop falling until the glut shrinks."

I ruefully note that only a few decades ago the *Times* was praising the *clergy* for warning us of imminent shortages of all natural resources, especially oil and gas. See *The Club of Rome* and *The 2000 Report to the President* (Jimmy Carter). I am also old enough to remember the panic when many gas stations ran out of gas in the Carter years, and Jimmy put on his cardigan sweater to lecture the nation on conserving resources. (I also remember the gas lines disappearing under President Reagan.)

Now I note Barack, when not golfing in Hawaii and adding to his carbon footprint, is lecturing us on climate change. And Pope Francis, too, when not flying to South America or Africa, is preaching to get us to "reduce our consumption" in order to help the poor and save the Earth.

So it goes.

Which gets me to politics. Democrats are shedding crocodile tears about the imminent death of the Republican Party at the hands of Donald Trump and Ted Cruz. My bet is that the Democratic Party is in more danger from a deeper split between Bernie Sanders and John Holdren. Socialist and super-progressive Bernie is giving Hillary fits in the Democratic primary.

Holdren leads the Greens and is chief science adviser to the president. As such, he is arguably more powerful than Senator Sanders.

Each lead movements that are incompatible. Progressives like Sanders and Clinton want economic growth and expect to rely on heavier taxes from a booming Wall Street to get more for the common man. Greens, like Holdren, want the opposite—to slow down or stop growth in order to save resources. They also want to control population growth in order to stall climate change.

The one issue they unite on is inequality. But neither recognizes that inequality, which prizes above all diversity of talents, is essential to economies *and* ecosystems. (To confirm this truth, I suggest a visit to Cuba and China: Cuba for a glance at what happens in a radically poor, badly polluted but equal society; China for what happens when you turn to a rich, market-driven, and more diverse unequal economy.)

....

I don't believe in reincarnation, but I did write the following poem, which I consider one of my best. It is also from my 1971 book, *a little while aware.*

> when I return will the fish still swim
> glide dive and slowly turn
> in the far-off deep-down sea
> will life still explode in seed and spore
> and decay in time
> will questions of great moment
> still be settled by childhood dreams and luck
> I think I shall return as rock
> my rhythm shall be paced slow
> to the grand tread
> of the century's boot
> I will be soil and trees, sparrows and snakes
> blue-bottomed whales, oak-ribbed barns
> skyscrapers too, but not too soon.

then when autumn returns again
I will have learned my piece
I will stand by my seat
and yes, I'll answer, yes

The Long Christmas Dinner

• • •

Apr. 18, 2016

A MADISON AUTHOR, THORNTON WILDER, grew up a few blocks down Gilman Street from our house. He wrote many plays, including the popular tear-jerker *Our Town* and the one-act *The Long Christmas Dinner*.

I directed both with high-school actors many years ago. *The Long Christmas Dinner* tells a brief but moving family story of a ninety-year-long Christmas dinner in an old Victorian house (similar to our house on Gilman Street, or so I like to fantasize). The house, just built by newlyweds Lucia and Roderick Bayard, is featured in the beginning of the play. As they sit down for their first Christmas dinner, an aging Grandmother Bayard in her wheelchair says, "I can remember when there were still Indians on this very ground, and I wasn't a young girl, either. I can remember when we had to cross the Mississippi on a new-made raft. I can remember when St. Louis and Kansas City were full of Indians."

The daughter, Lucia, breezily replies to her mother, "Imagine that! What a wonderful day for our first Christmas dinner; a beautiful sunny morning, snow, splendid sermon. Dr. McCarthy preaches a splendid sermon. I cried and cried." Lucia later follows up with a comment often repeated by other family members as they age and disappear: "Every least twig is wrapped with ice. You almost never see that."

Mother Bayard soon mysteriously disappears from the table to be replaced by husbands and wives, uncles, cousins, daughters, sons, granddaughters, and grandsons.

It broke me up when my wife, Jane, said much the same thing as Lucia as she looked out the window of our hundred-year-old Gilman Street house on an unseasonably cold April morning: "Look! The twigs in the backyard are all covered with ice. It's beautiful."

And then when I reread the play script this morning to write this blog, I broke up again into still more tears!

The play goes on to tell homely stories about the house and the Bayard family occupants as they age and disappear. By the end, only a granddaughter, Genevieve, lives in the house with an aging cousin, Ermengarde, who has no place to go after retiring from the first grade she taught for many years. Genevieve says to her cousin before she, too, exits, "I can stand everything but this terrible soot everywhere. We should have moved long ago. We're surrounded by factories. We have to change the window curtains every week."

The old Ermengarde is left alone to remark, "I don't see why the rest of you dislike it. I like it more than I can say."

It's really not quite like that on Gilman Street now. True, Jane and I are aging, and both of us will soon disappear, but our lovely house will go on and be okay. Factories do not surround it. It is across the street from the former governor of Wisconsin's mansion in the middle of a historical district that is protected from demolition by city ordinances. As in the play, our lovely house may be taken over by one of Jane's children, Samuel, and his lovely family (if he can manage to buy out the rest of our joint children and their families who stand to inherit it).

The tears made me think, too, of Emily's speech again (delivered in my high-school directing days by the daughter of a dear friend who died just a few weeks ago). Emily, too, dies in act one of *Our Town*. She returns from the dead to have the justifiably famous speech. (As I may have said before, I'm a big crybaby for this one, too.)

Oh, Mama, look at me one minute as though you really saw me. Mama, fourteen years have gone by. I'm dead. You're a grandmother, Mama! Wally's dead, too. His appendix burst on a camping trip to North Conway. We felt just terrible about it—don't you remember? But, just for a moment now we're all together. Mama, just for a moment we're happy. Let's really look at one another!... I can't. I can't go on. It goes so fast. We don't have time to look at one another. I didn't realize. So all that was going on and we never noticed. Take me back—up the hill—to my grave. But first: Wait! One more look. Good-bye, Good-bye world. Good-bye, Grover's Corners...Mama and Papa. Good-bye to clocks ticking... and Mama's sunflowers. And food and coffee. And new ironed dresses and hot baths...and sleeping and waking up. Oh, earth, you are too wonderful for anybody to realize you. Do any human beings ever realize life while they live it—every, every minute?

The omniscient narrator answers Emily, "No. (pause)...The saints and poets, maybe they do some."

Good News and Bad News on Labor Day

• • •

Sept, 5, 2016

THE GOOD NEWS IS THAT I am alive and kicking. (Not with a very strong kick though. I missed last week's blog because I had a nasty case of lumbar radiculopathy, extra-strength sciatica for short. I also broke my nose in a kitchen fall. This and other recent falls combined with difficulty in computer typing led to my bad news as well.)

The bad news, as my 90th birthday nears in a few days, it's time to retire these blogs.

As to Labor Day, I celebrate by working. As usual. As a teacher, like many of my fellow teachers, there were always papers to grade, lessons to plan, classes to attend, students to help, (and for science teachers) labs to clean up. As an entrepreneur there were always more scripts to write, more video to take and find, more programs to edit, more bills to pay, more government regulations to pay attention to, more countries to visit, and a pile of other work that all business managers must cope with. As an old man there were always more books to read, more philosophic thinking to do, and more weekly blogs to write. (I have to admit I was a bit stung last week that I got zero email complaints when I was not able to keep up my weekly blog. I got the message and am suspending the blog writing for now.)

As to working on Labor Day I'm not asking for sympathy because it has always been my choice. For the most part it has been a good choice—on occasion, a thrilling one. Many, if not most, teachers, artists, scientists, musicians, and self-employed people, who rarely or never take a day off, know what I'm talking about. You get immersed in a work that is rewarding and find the fun of making a living more interesting than weekend and vacation fun and games. In fact the latter get downright boring.

I am sad to leave you this Labor Day but there is a time for everything and for me that time has arrived.

Bill Stonebarger, Owner/President Hawkhill

P. S. Arrogantly I do think that I have made a unique contribution to the world in my blogs. I am struggling now to proofread my latest and probably last book, *Bill's Blogs*. It is a collection of what I consider my best blogs over the past few years. Not a model of modesty, I predict that *Bill's Blogs* will *eventually* (it may take as much as fifty or so years) turn out to be a classic.

www.ingramcontent.com/pod-product-compliance
Lightning Source LLC
Chambersburg PA
CBHW071458040426
42444CB00008B/1402